# Naming For Power

*Creating Successful Names for the Business World*

# NASEEM JAVED

**LINKBRIDGE PUBLISHING** • **NEW YORK** • **TORONTO**

**LINKBRIDGE PUBLISHING**
New York – Toronto


Library of Congress Cataloging-in-Publication Data.


Javed, Naseem
Naming For Power:
Creating Successful Names for The Business World
C.I.P. 93-80799


**ISBN 0-9639702-0-8**

Printed in Canada
December, 1993
First Edition

# Naming For Power

This book is dedicated
to my mother, Amtul,
my wife, Lucie,
my son, Tashi.

Also, to the twenty-six
letters of the alphabet,
especially the letters
A,B, and C, which
taught me a great deal.

**Naseem Javed**, president of ABC Namebank International, is a highly-profiled specialist in the creation and development of unique, powerful names. Naseem is experienced in naming newly merged or acquired companies, implementing corporate name changes, developing brand names for new products, technologies or services, as well as evaluating and auditing names already in use. Many of his trend-setting ideas have been widely published and broadcast throughout North America.

Javed founded ABC Namebank International in New York and Toronto, which is now a leading name development company. Over a 15-year period, ABC has built a solid track record in providing creative names which are highly suitable to marketing goals and equally available for worldwide registration.

ABC Namebank has focused on helping Fortune 500 companies and other leadership corporations on a wide variety of naming issues.

Clients include: IBM, General Motors, Telus, Honeywell, Bell Canada, Texaco, BellSouth, Ford, Magna, HealthTrust, Johnson & Johnson, Molson, Sasktel, Air Canada, NOVA, GENNUM, AGT, RadioShack, Petro-Canada, GENEXXA, Expotel, MINNOVA, Peat Marwick KPMG, CARA, Woolworth, QUNO, DairyWorld, Merck, BBDO Worldwide, and CELESTICA.

# CONTENTS

**INTRODUCTION**

**1**   **NAMES IN MOTION: CARS**          19

TRAFFIC JAMS OF THE MIND          24

ALPHABET, AND NUMBER, SOUPS          33

DRIVING YOUR CAR TO COURT          35

ILL-CHOSEN NAMES          37

**2**   **INTERNAL NAMING**          41

THE BIG  PICTURE-TYPE
PERSONALITY:          44

THE SCIENTIST-TYPE
PERSONALITY:          46

THE ROMANTIC-TYPE PERSONALITY:          47

THE ENGLISH-ONLY TYPE
PERSONALITY:          48

THE O.K.-TYPE PERSONALITY:          49

THE TECHNO-TYPE PERSONALITY:          50

THE STRATEGIC-TYPE:
A COMPOSITE          51

**3**   **FOCUS GROUPIES**                      53

    CONTESTS WHERE EVERYONE
    LOSES                              57

    FOCUS GROUPS DON'T WORK            61

**4**   **NAMING BUSINESS DREAMS:**
    **SURNAMES**                       67

    FROM ADAM'S GARDEN TO
    KRAFT'S FOOD                       71

    TO SURNAMES WITH LOVE              75

    FAMILIES HAVE PROBLEMS, TOO        78

    A BULL IN A CHINA SHOP             82

**5**

**NAMING BUSINESS DREAMS:
GEOGRAPHIC NAMES**      85

STRANGE, UNKNOWN VILLAGES      88

LUBRICATING COMPANY NAMES      90

**CASE STUDY :**
COINING A NAME TO ESCAPE
GEOGRAPHY      91

BANKING ON NAMES      93

**CASE STUDY:**
FROM WESTERN CANADA TO
THE ENTIRE WORLD      96

GEOGRAPHIC NAMES ARE RAPIDLY
DROPPING OFF THE MAP      100

**6**

**NAMING BUSINESS DREAMS:
DESCRIPTIVE AND/OR
DICTIONARY NAMES:**      103

WASTING NAMES      111

**CASE STUDY:**
GETTING THE MAXIMUM
OUT OF A DICTIONARY NAME      113

IN CONCLUSION. . . .      115

**7**  **NAMING BUSINESS DREAMS:**
       **COINED NAMES**                        117

       **CASE STUDY:**
       A BRAND NEW NAME FOR
       AN OLD INSTITUTION                      124

       A NAME THAT DIDN'T FLY                  126

**8**  **NAMING SPECTRUM**                     129

       NAMING HANGOVERS                        141

       NAMING GAMES                            142

       NAMING GENDERS                          144

       NAMING ECOLOGY                          148

       ROCKY NAMES                             150

       NAMING GOLD                             151

       NAMING FUNCTIONS                        153

**9**

**THE HIGHS AND LOWS
OF HI-TECH NAMING**      155

**CASE STUDY:**
RE-ENGINEERING OF
ENGINEERING SUCCESS      162

THE DAWN OF HI-TECH NAMING      164

WHAT IS YOURS,
MAY WELL BE MINE!      169

THE UPPER AND LOWER-CASE
DISEASE OF TECHIES      170

CONFUSION EVERYWHERE--
EVEN AT I.B.M.      171

COMPARING APPLES...
TO APRICOTS??      174

BUGS IN THE FORBIDDEN FRUIT      176

SO HOW SHOULD ONE NAME
A HI-TECH COMPANY, PRODUCT
OR SERVICE?      178

**CASE STUDY:**
SHACKS, HUTS, AND TENTS      181

THE FUTURE OF HI-TECH
NAMING                                    183

**CASE STUDY:**
ACCOUNTING FOR A NEW NAME        184

**10**    **NOVO-CONSUMERISM**             189

WHAT ABOUT THOSE
"STORE BRANDS"?                           192

WHAT ABOUT STORE
LABEL FASHIONS?                           198

BRAND NAMES:  WORTH
FIGHTING FOR?                             204

GREAT BRAND NAMES:  WORTH
THEIR WEIGHT IN GOLD                      208

DON'T FIGHT THEM--BUY THEM!!              210

**11**    **CUSTODY OF A NAME**             215

RINGS OF FIRE                             219

THE GLORIOUS SPIN-OFF VALUE
OF RECOGNIZABLE BRAND NAMES               222

GOOD BRAND NAMES--
LIKE DIAMONDS                             224

**12**     **WHERE DO WE GO
FROM HERE?**     229

NAMING INFLUENCES     232

RENAMING TO ELIMINATE AN
EXISTING IDENTITY PROBLEM     235

EVALUATING EXISTING NAMES     237

ON-GOING NAME DEVELOPMENT
STRATEGIES     239

AND IN CONCLUSION...     241

SOME FINAL THOUGHTS     242

**ANNOTATED BIBLIOGRAPHY**     243

**INDEX**     249

## INTRODUCTION

Just what **is** the role of a business name in our society?

Anything you have purchased during the past week--the clothes you're wearing, the cologne you use; the car you drive; the computer you work on; the watch you wear; the soup you eat-- even including the purchase of this book--were all affected because of the influence of a name! And that goes for the company you work for, and the street you live on, as well.

A good name means high satisfaction for the end- user, and power for the business which carries it.

Names are like weapons: Marketing weapons, which have one main function: To come to the mind of a buyer at the time of a purchasing decision. Otherwise, why bother naming at all? You can simply use a number: Company 829 selling Product Number 311*plus*.

Unless you have already experienced it, sooner or later, you will arrive in a position where you will be faced with a critical decision to name something strategic in your company.

It is important for you to know that, several times every minute, 24 hours a day, seven days a week, a new name gets registered somewhere around the globe.

If you, personally, were involved in naming, say, your company's newsletter, or a small software program, you most probably will be **lost** in a **major** naming exercise, unless you have ways to handle it. This is because few people have ever been involved in a serious naming issue.

Today, if your business--whether big or small, local or global, with a  product or service--has a poor name, it will quickly be on the fast track to oblivion.

Now, read on.  And welcome to the very real, very complex, very **essential** world of naming.

# Names in Motion: Cars

## 1

By the year 2000 there will be some one thousand different makes and models of the cars on the road worldwide.

If cars are the second most important--and expensive--purchase decision after buying a house, then don't you think the name of that valuable asset is crucial?

*ne recent morning, I was ushered into a large boardroom of a major automobile manufacturer in Detroit. The problem was quickly obvious: The final choice of a name for a vitally important new car product had not only failed to hit the public; it had just hit the fan.*

The management was very upset, and everyone in the room was pacing back and forth like an investment company the day after Black Monday.

One should note here: **This chaotic scene is repeated countless times a day in major corporations around the world.**

A list of candidates for the bouncing baby pet car was ceremoniously brought out, from which the hopeful final name would be selected. One need not be a writer for **Saturday Night Live** or **David Letterman** to guess what was on the sheet.

The first list consisted of a row of names of the
twelve zodiac signs. This was followed by a long
row of all the famous mountains in
North America. Then came Indian tribes.
(After the controversy of the infamous, racist
"Tomahawk chop" at the Atlanta Braves baseball
games, and the grinning-idiot cigar-store Indian
mascot of the Cleveland Indians, one wonders
about that one a bit.)

Then a long list of Rivers:
NILE. NIGER. RHINE. MISSISSIPPI.
List of Deserts:
SAHARA. NAVAJO.
List of Trees:
BANYON. REDWOOD. PINE. OAK. BIRCH.
List of Mammals:
BADGER. CAMEL. CARIBOU.
List of Seashells:
CONCH. CLAM. MUSSELS. SCALLOPS.
List of Seabirds:
GULL. TERN. LOON. PIPER.
List of Reptiles:
CROCODILE. COPPERHEAD.
And so on. . .

The natural reaction of the participants was:
How on earth did they forget to add the names of
butterflies? Fish from both seas and oceans?
Insects? Flowers? After all, the **Ford Shark**
might prove irresistible to lawyers. And the
**Chrysler Praying Mantis** could attract both
religious types **and** Mafia enforcers.

**QUADRICYCLE**

Name of the first
car developed by
Henry Ford in
1896.

21

The problem was clear, even to the uninspired potential car-namers:  The purportedly "romantic" names of famous rivers and mountains have long been used, and not only for automobiles, but in many auto-related--and totally unrelated, and often highly dubious--areas. (A name like the FORD MISSISSIPPI, for example, or the GM WYOMING, may not call forth any positive imagery for Japanese or British consumers.)

And off they went, moving down each long and tedious list, slashing away like the killer in the **Nightmare on Elm Street** series.   The horror **here** was, only the most unpronounceable, utterly obscure, and seriously confusing names were eventually left on the page.

In total desperation, only one of these many hundreds of names had survived the endless selection process--and this was **after** the local office (in conjunction with offices around the world) had exchanged **over 600 faxes** (!) in this seemingly romantic, more often than not trivial, pursuit.

The grumbling around the room was audible as the ultimate decision was being finalized in Asia. And--not surprisingly--my company was invited to "quickly come up with a name solution, preferably within a couple of days."

"A couple of days"--for a car which had cost many hundreds of millions to design and manufacture, and which would both directly as well as indirectly affect the earnings of hundreds of thousands of men and women (and the payments on their mortgages; and the education of their children), right around the globe!

In this case, unfortunately, time had run out. There was nothing I could do for this car.

The eventual name that was chosen satisfied few who sat and paced in that room that depressing afternoon. It is now on the road, true; but it has an alpha-numeric name (a few letters and a few numbers mixed together) which is lost in the crowd, and reminds me, as I pass it on the road, what a great opportunity had been missed.

And this was the car which hoped to be sold around the world to people who speak over 1,000 languages and live in over 100 countries (**and counting**, thanks to the collapse of communism and the rise of neo-nationalism and ethnicity).

### RAMBLER

Thomas Jeffrey was a successful manufacturer of bicycles under this name before moving into automobile manufacturing.

## TRAFFIC JAMS OF THE MIND

What have automobile manufacturers done with the names of their cars, when they (presumably) hope to make their vehicle stand out majestically from the competition?

In the lifetime of every person reading these words, one could count car names on the fingers of both hands. By the year 2000, there will be **over one thousand** different makes and models and brands of cars around the world.

In the 1960s, one could create a car and give it the moniker "Mustang" or "Cougar" and do quite well. But to give you an idea of the problem facing the industry today, let us make our own list for a moment, thanks to a recent (and strikingly distinct and uncreative) name trend for cars on the roads today.

Do you see a pattern here? Hell, a visually-challenged person could detect the pattern! Sadly, car makers have become so possessed by the Japanese-sounding letter "A," that there is now a jungle of almost-identical, ever-more-confusing car names on the road today.

Names of Cars on the Road Today.

**ACURA**
**ASUNA**
**ALTIMA**
**ACHIEVA**
**AURORA**
**FESTIVA**
**INTEGRA**
**ELANTRA**
**PRECIDIA**
**MAXIMA**
**SONATA**
**SAMARA**
**SERENIA**
**SENTRA**
**LUMINA**
**CORSICA**

This is the result of a dumb, cheap, low-intelligent hi-tech computer generation of names, often accompanied by focus groups. It is so obvious, one would **think** that the managers of companies totaling over a trillion dollars would have grasped it by now:

Such over-use has created a kind of "name pollution," making it extremely difficult for consumers to distinguish one brand from another--which, one would think, is the main purpose of naming a product in the first place. Hundreds of millions of dollars are spent yearly to draw attention to the names of their products, yet this bombardment is probably creating more confusion than recognition in the marketplace.

The recent obsession with the letter "A" is only a later pattern in the naming of cars, as the following historical view will show.

In the earliest decades of the industry, Henry put out models "A," "B," "C," "F," "K," "N," "R," "S," and the wildly successful "T" on the roads of North America, even if the only color you could get was black.

The nearly-as-daring Oldsmobile (literally) cranked out its own Model "A," "F," and "H," and Series "M," "Z," and "X."

Chrysler, even before the creative Mr. Iacocca took over (indeed, possibly making it **necessary** for Mr. Iacocca to come in and save the company), created the "B-70," the "F-58," the "G70" and the "E80."

One wonders if the public felt it necessary to obtain their flying permit as well as a driver's license, before setting foot inside a Chrysler automobile.

Yet, once the early days of letters (and numbers) had seemed to pass into history-- think of Mazda's 626, for just one more recent example-- there was an explosion of zodiac, astro-celestial and zoological sources. (True, Ransom Ellie Olds founded a successful firm; as did David Dunbar Buick and Walter P. Chrysler. Not to mention Henry Ford.)

And over in Europe, Carl Benz and Enzol Ferrari and Andre Citroen did quite well using their own (now-renowned and accepted) names--with the occasional inspired move, such as that of Nicola Romeo, who created a catchy first name for his product from the tongue-defying "**Anonima Lombardo Fabrica Automobili**," which most prefer to just call "Alfa" for short.)

Most Americans know if they are an Aries or a Taurus--or if they **drive** one, for that matter. But for well over a billion Chinese around the world, the zodiac is divided into roosters, dogs, horses and oxen.

True, their Rabbit is the luckiest of signs, and that has already been grabbed by one automaker.

But how about the Chinese sign of the Pig? ("Affectionate and kind to loved ones.")  Or the Monkey?  ("Very intelligent and able to influence people.")  Or the Rat?  ("Ambitious and honest.")

Then again, the Pig **is** considered vile and unclean by a half-billion Muslims and several million Jews, so that could prove to be a problem. And the Cow, so holy and sensitive to hundreds of millions in India, could end up causing further concern.

But how could the Chinese **resist** the Ford or Chevrolet "Dog"??  ("Honest and loyal leader of men.")  The reality of hundreds of millions of Chinese declaring proudly that "my new car is a **Dog**!" could add a whole new twist to automobile criticism.

Let us recall, then, Ford's partiality for animals with high horsepower: Bronco. Cougar.  Lynx. And, more recently, the astro-zoological Taurus. (The cusp of Aries having been taken, one assumes.  Yet for some reason, the **equally** legitimate sign of Cancer has never caught on with the auto-buying public.)

## MERCEDES

Mercedes Jelinek was the granddaughter of Delmer Benz, the founder of the company.

## TOYOTA

Toyoda Automatic Loom Works was the original name of the company.

Family names can occasionally be disastrous, as the once-tragic, now-comical name of "Edsel" quickly illustrates. (The early, journalistic description, "The front of the car looks like an Oldsmobile sucking on a lemon" will probably live far longer then the car itself.)

There have been crystal-clear images of power, such as the Mustang and Charger. There have been images of luxurious ride and expensive craftsmanship which have all successfully been burned into our brains and our highways, from Continental to Imperial to Fleetwood.
Yet even names with obscure origins have occasionally caught on with the public. Witness the initials following the great Pontiac of the 60s: The GTO. One wonders if one purchaser in ten thousand knew (or knows today) that the name stands for "Grand Turismo Omologato," and was borrowed from a racing Ferrari. Or that the last word originally meant the European beauty had been "approved for racing," or "homologated." In the States, all the dealers and public cared about was that the car was built for speed and power--and the initials stuck.

Should we care that Toyota's MR2 stands for "Mid-engine Runabout 2-seater"? Do we **have** to know that Mercedes-Benz' renowned 560SEL reflects total honesty? The 560 tells us that the car has a 5.6 liter V-8 engine; the "S" means the firm's finest class of automobiles; the"E" is from the German word for fuel-injection ("Einspritzung"); and the "L" stands for "long wheel base."

As the salesman used to tell us, "If you have to ask the price, you can't afford it."

Mercury, of course, was the speedy messenger of the gods of ancient Greek religion, even if nobody believes that anymore.  And Mazda is a god of light in its home country of Japan, which probably never moved any American toward purchasing the product.

**MITSUBISHI**

This means "Three Diamonds" in Japanese.

Did you know that "LETTUCE," "ESCARGOT," and "CAPPUCINO" are all models of cars named in Japan?  Of course, in that culture, lettuce has the image of "layers of protection" and escargot, for a small delivery truck, suggests safety and reliability.

Some names--like office buildings--**scream** their post-war origin, and have become almost comically "dated" today.

In the 1950s, Chevrolet had Turfmaster, Loadmaster and Jobmaster--names which we would laugh off (instead of drive off) the lot, four decades later.  And what of Chrysler's Flightomatic?  And how about Jetaway Hydromatic Drive, Miracle Edge-Power, Velvet Pressure, Jumbodrum Brakes, Touchomatic, Roadguide Fender, Vacomatic, and so many more?

Understandingly, manufacturers who treat the exercise of naming their cars without deliberate thought, and ignore scientific methods, risk marketing disaster.

## LA FEMME

In 1955, Chrysler introduced a model, complete with comb, compact, lipsticks, purses, etc., all in pink, designed for the female audience. It survived only two years.

Our favorite (and perhaps yours as well) occurred when GM discovered that its "Nova" was simply not moving well in Spanish-speaking markets. Maybe if they had hired more Hispanics in their marketing division, they would have known that "No-Va" means "no go" to any four-year-old child in Spain, Mexico--or New York City and Los Angeles, for that matter.

It's a very funny anecdote, but it is redolent with meaning for any automobile manufacturer who hopes to sell his product on the world market. And let us never forget that the much-loved "Body by Fisher" of GM fame ended up being translated overseas as "Corpse by Fisher."

Other stories are almost as instructive: West German dealers had to be scraped off the roof when they were abruptly informed that Rolls-Royce had (already!) named a new model "Silver Mist," since "mist" in the German language is a colloquial expression which means "manure." Similarly, but less fragrantly, French car-sellers insisted on Chevrolet's withdrawing the "Chevette," because it means "horse," which has the wrong connotation for a car in that land.

And--possibly best of all, and even most disastrous--let us treasure the moment when Ford renamed its "Meteor" model "Caliente" for South America, without taking the trouble of asking anyone living on that continent if the term has any dangerous connotation there.

It does.  "Caliente" is slang for "hooker" for tens of millions of potential buyers in South America; an interesting evening, perhaps, but **not** the kind of car you wish to buy for your wife, husband, son or daughter.

If linguistic **faux pas** and (often) subtle nuances do not trip up a car manufacturer, then litigation sure can.  After all, car makers--like everyone else who has created anything for anyone beyond their immediate family--are up against the inescapable fact that there are countless names which have been legally registered around the world.

So as many of you will recall, when Toyota launched its upscale "Lexus" line, everything was brought to a skidding halt because the name was legally challenged by a global information company based in the United States called "Lexus Data."

With **a new car model being introduced every single day**, the battle for the minds of several billion potential customers has become heated. And the advent of international marketing has meant a **far greater** struggle for domination of steadily narrower market segments.
Marketers have been scrambling about for **any** advantage to seek distinction over their competitors, be it in the realm of speed, style, handling, new technology, functionality or color.

## REGAL

Buick, Dodge, and Studebaker each had a model called Regal.

31

**But what they often fail to comprehend is that, in the end, to evoke the proper image there must be a name created which the customers will be able to relate to!**

## BUT COULD JOHN DELOREON SLAM DUNK?

Michael Jordan may have quit pro basketball, but his name could live forever on the sides of cars, if Chicagoland Chevy dealers have their way. In late 1993, they announced plans to bring out a commemorative-edition Michael Jordan Blazer sport-utility vehicle. The cars will have a special grill, 24-karat gold "Blazer" emblems, and a brass plaque sporting Jordan's signature. May it do better than the Edsel!

I believe that one indication of the auto industry's poor attention to the development of good names is the plethora of alpha-numeric combinations, only hinted at by the absurd abundance of "A's" which were noted earlier.

## ALPHABET, AND NUMBER, SOUPS

One can trace this trend quite easily:  The success which Nissan (then called Datsun in North America) had in the early 1970s with its 240Z sports car.  (Today, one can purchase a Nissan **300ZX**, which is almost meaningless; true, the "3" refers to its 3-liter engine, but the "Z" and the "X" are admitted by their own namers as "nothing more than sporty letters.")

So, while a handful of serious car enthusiasts might be able to relate to such numbers and letters--a minuscule percentage of the total market, I'm sure--the vast majority of consumers cannot make heads or tails out of the difference between an NS-X, an RX-7, an XR4Ti, a 24KOSX, an MX-6, an SHD, or any other monstrosity.  Although German readers might be thrilled to discover that the Mercury XR4Ti comes from the German for "Mercury"; the "X" means "sporty";  the "R" means rear-wheel drive; the "4" refers to its number of cylinders; its "T" stands for turbocharged, and the sweet lower-case "i"  obviously means fuel-injected.

(We have no doubt that you are reaching for your credit card this very moment to purchase one.)

The problem is, in coming up with all these seemingly eye-catching combinations, car makers still have not solved the all-important **international identity problem.**

### FAIRLADY Z

This is the name given to the Datsun 240Z in Japan.

## CADILLAC

Antoine De Lamarque Cadillac was the founder of the company.

A simple example: <u>English</u> alpha-numerics do **not** translate equally, or convey the same ear-catching power, in other countries; for instance, "240Z" reads "Descientos Cuarenta Zeta" in Spanish. One may as well drive a no-go auto and try to pick up a horse or a hooker.

**Successful names have always given consumers something to grab hold of.**
The famous "Arrow" was named to convey the distinctive shape of that car's pointed chrome bumper, and it did so. "Jeep" was directly derived from the U.S. Army's abbreviation for G.P., which in turn came from "General Purpose Vehicle," and boy, did it stick in the world's collective consciousness!

## DRIVING YOUR CAR TO COURT

One strange example of the proprietary nature of names recently occurred in Alpine, Wyoming, which has a population of only 97, but where "Jeep's Bar" **still** caught the attention of Chrysler Motors.  The slightly larger automobile company threatened its owner Jeep Molnar in 1989, insisting that his "corporate name is a violation of Federal Law," since "Jeep" is now a registered trademark of Jeep Eagle Corp., a Chrysler subsidiary.

Mr. Molnar, born Fred but nicknamed Jeep by his father as a baby (after a minor character in a Popeye cartoon of the 1930s), might still be fighting Chrysler over their demands (no franchising his bar; adding "bar and lounge" after its name, etc.)

Clearly, even a personally-named bar in a tiny midwestern town can seem problematic for a billion-dollar company that wishes to protect its brand names.

### Volvo Cars and Ladies?

How on earth can a Swedish car and a Chinese "hostess bar" become confused--or litigious?

Easily.  Back in 1990, the owners of one of Hong Kong's largest "hostess bars" chose to call itself Club Volvo.

### NISSAN

Datsun became Nissan in 1984, as it planned to surpass 700,000 sales for the first time.  It had to change signs at 1,100 dealerships, with a total of nearly 5,000 signs worldwide.  A change of this nature can cost 50-100 million dollars.

**ISUZU**

This means
"Fifty Bells"
in Japanese.

This did not rest well with the clean-cut, family automobile firm of Volvo in Sweden, which promptly sued the Chinese firm for "damaging its reputation for building high-quality family cars."

It is still in the courts, at the time of this writing. Still, it is interesting to note that in Asia, the image of Volvo is **not** "family car," but rather a glamorous status symbol which actually rivals Mercedes.  So maybe the image of customers shelling out over $77 (U.S.) an hour to get a lovely young woman to join them for a drink might be **good** for Volvo's image--at least in the Far East.

## ILL-CHOSEN NAMES

In 1989, SUZUKI released its low-priced SWIFT in Canada.  One automobile critic noted that it had "a fairly cramped interior, almost no luggage space, high noise levels, a bouncy ride"--but then, they were promising **speed** with that name, not anything else.

Of course, poorly-thought-out names can be threatening, rather than life-saving:  After a rave review of Honda's upmarket Acura line's 5-cylinder "Vigor," one critic concluded by quoting a woman in his office:  "I would be a little embarrassed to say I had a Vigor.  It just sounds like an odd name for a car.  Too male, too macho!"  Noting that "the lady was by no means alone," the automobile critic went on to protest, "It is a pity such a fine car may have to overcome a name that has such a negative connotation for many people."

Indeed it is.

In November, 1991, GM Europe began to turn out a low-cost entry named FRONTERA.  The right-hand-drive ones for Britain were the first to be produced, followed by left-hand-drive models for the Continent, a few months later.  It's nice to see that American automobile manufacturers have finally noticed that different countries often drive on different sides of the road.  But as for that name. . .

**CHRYSLER**

Walter P. Chrysler was the founder of the firm.

## CATCHY NAMES ARE NEVER EASY

In late 1993, Mazda Motor barely beat out GM's Oldsmobile in chosing their latest car name.

While Olds had whittled its endless search down to two names, Millenia and Aurora, Mazda had already trademarked the former. And so, 1994 will see the new Mazda Millenia, while GM will be driving the Oldsmobile Aurora.

Piagga company created an agile little scooter which hummed sweetly as it flew though the busy, narrow streets of Italy and the rest of Europe, its name "Vespa" (meaning "wasp"), was easy to relate to.

And the long love affair between the States and the small-model Volkswagen, which came so soon after the guns stopped blasting between Yanks and Germans, was based on the strong, powerful, yet compact image of the "beetle." Chysler's latest , speedy sportscar, Viper, has a widely-understood name for North America. However, outside North America, it carries no connotation of a powerful, rapidly-moving snake.

To gain a **real** edge in the market, clever auto makers will have to devote an increasing amount of resources to the development of names: Names which evoke strong images and are memorable, transportable to other cultures and languages, and are proprietory.   With these attributes, the name will become valuable --no, invaluable--assets to each car's success in the global market.

Auto makers, like any successful marketer, **must** come to understand that **they have to adopt a disciplined approach to name development,** and one which requires an appreciation of a name's strategic value, and a deep understanding of how a name can be properly treated, and legally protected.

All too often--I recall that frantic, idiotic meeting which I attended with a major car manufacturer, described in the opening paragraph of this chapter--name development is left as an ad hoc process, attended to at random (!)   While millions upon millions of dollars are eagerly and legitimately spent on the planning, manufacturing, introducing and promoting new models of cars, **shockingly little is invested to insure a consistent and effective way of naming them!**

Billions of men, women and children read newspapers and watch TV; they are bombarded with many thousands of product names every day, and can **hardly** be expected to differentiate among dozens of vehicles which all sound alike, whether Altima or Achieva or Asuna or Sonata or Sentra or. . .

*Back in 1905, a promising young company named Rolls-Royce introduced a car which could not exceed 20 miles per hour.*
*It was named "**Legal Limit**."*
*Where is the guy who thought that up, now that we need him?*

# Internal Naming

## 2

Managers who do
their jobs well
may not be able to
**name** as well.

*ames are often developed internally, within an organization.  No matter how one tries to name a major product, a service, or even the company itself, certain components are unavoidable.  And whether some of the key candidate names are positive or negative, one can only be sure after the final results are tabulated.  Here is the traditional scenario:*

A new name issue starts as a hush-hush decision, often from the very top, whether the C.E.O. or the project management team.  They have often  all gone through a long period of incubation, and idealistic soul-searching.  The top man finally has the answer--the whole game plan is figured out-- and the war room is ready.  Everything is ready to go.

The prototype, the brochure, the endless
press conferences; you name it--but **there is no
name.** True, there is a secret project code name.
And a floating list of ideas. But no final name
has been chosen.

At this stage, most companies attempt to find
the new name through an internal exercise.
Now let us look at the psychological implications
of the internal naming exercise, whether in a
small dynamic company, or a major **Fortune 500**
corporation.

The law of Nature dictates that, if you have ten
managers sitting in a boardroom, you will have at
least ten distinct personalities--and with good
reason; it would be eerie to have all ten of then
behaving and thinking alike! Here is a general
breakdown of these top characterizations which
often emerge in any naming exercise. (If you
doubt the following, please try it on your own;
you will soon see similar actions at play.)

For the sake of practicality, and the length of this
book, I have extracted only certain personalities,
and their reactions, specifically toward a Naming
Issue, and have left the rest of this fearful
Pandora's Box undisturbed:

## THE BIG PICTURE-TYPE PERSONALITY:

This person has a "view from the high rise"; a general overview of the marketplace. This person likes Big Talk, to go with the Big Picture. This old school individual is locked into quarterly performances, and merger and acquisitions-style management. At this point, the name must convey everything which the company does.

For example:

- INTERCONSOLIDATED AMALGAMATED CORPORATION.

- DE-AMALGAMATED INTERDIVERSIFIED INTERCONTINENTALIZED INC.

- SUPERPOWER CORPORATION

- MULTICORP INC.

This type would create the longest names in human history, which would look stunning on the Magna Carta, or at least on the American Declaration of Independence, but not necessarily pleasant on the side of a floppy disk. In this person's most extreme moods, one will hear such names recommended as:

- OPERATION THUNDERBOLT INC.

- PEOPLE'S ADVANTAGE CORPORATION

● FUTURE NOW INCORPORATED.
This last company, now the 10th fastest growing
firm in America today, most probably would **not**
call itself PAST THEN LIMITED!

At this stage of the naming exercise, while the
project is on the table, all the questions and
answers are in the air. Everybody is excited and
wants to have a winning name by the end of the
meeting. And, of course, everyone has an idea
on what to call it.

Let's look at the following names of leading
corporations of today, which were most probably
named by the Big Picture-Type:

● AMERICAN POWER CONVERSION

● AMERICAN WASTE SERVICES

● CONTINENTAL MEDICAL SERVICES

● MEDICAL CARE AMERICA

● QUANTUM HEALTH RESOURCES

● 20TH CENTURY INDUSTRIES

## THE SCIENTIST-TYPE PERSONALITY:

Thanks to a strong engineering background, this one feels as if a dazed look is sufficient.

This person suffers from a burden of scientific guilt, and a decent understanding of Darwin's evolutionary theory. This type has a mathematical attitude; requires proof before acting on anything; is cautious and sequential in both style and approach. Preferences would include:

- SONOTONICAL SYSTEM INC.
- ACCURATECH CORPORATION
- DURATRAMAUTIC LIMITED
- COMPRESSAPROBTECH INC.

Alas, the end user (read: consumer) would probably feel it necessary to take graduate courses in science before touching this product, out of fear that it would explode. In this person's most extreme moments, suggestions might include:

- INTERGALACTICOMA COMPANY
- IMMOBIOGENICA CORPORATION

**Good Luck.**
Famous companies of today named by the Scientist-Type include:

- SYBASE INC.
- SYQUEST TECHNOLOGY
- XILINX INC.

## THE ROMANTIC-TYPE PERSONALITY:

This person has two feet firmly on the ground, with head dancing above the clouds. Humming also helps. This type of personality strongly believes in romantic sincerity to the point that the customer must be touched by it. Everything must have an advantage, choice and something extra. The names flow freely from this one:

- PEOPLE'S CHOICE
- CUSTOMER'S CHOICE
- PROOF POSITIVE
- YOUR CHOICE
- VIEWER'S CHOICE
- NATURAL SYSTEM
- ADVANTAGE PLUS
- OCEAN SURF
- LIGHT N' EASY
- O 'LALA

In the extreme moments, the Romantic might come up with:

- ANUSOL
- ALL FIBER
- ECOTEK
- VAGISIL

Famous names of today, done by the Romantics:

- PROOF POSITIVE (a service of MCI)
- LASTING COLORS by LOVING CARE
- REQUEST Jeans

## THE ENGLISH-ONLY-TYPE PERSONALITY:

Here, one encounters Country Estate behavior;
a blazer, and a pronounced British accent.
This person radiates the sensibility of The Club,
The Courtyard, and The Good Old Days
of the Empire.

This one's preferences, naturally, would be:

- WILLOWDALE CASTLE
- MONARCH'S BLUE
- CORONATION
- MORNING GLORY
- BRIDAL PATH

Only roast beef from **this** naming participant;
don't look for either filet mignon or teriyaki from
this character. In an extreme case, the
English-Only-type might let loose with:

- CONQUEST OF ASIA
- SUN-NEVER-SETS UNLIMITED

Here come the days of glory!

More famous names in use today, clearly named
by the English-Only-Type:

- WELLPOINT (a service of BLUE CROSS)
- WELLFLEET COMMUNICATION
- U.S. LONG DISTANCE

## THE O.K.-TYPE PERSONALITY:

This person is Dale Carnegie in action;
everything is just fine, dandy and grand.
A firm handshake and a smile are both essential
and inevitable.

Everything is simple and O.K. to this person, and
his/her preferences would be:

- WASH 'N WEAR
- TRICK-O-TREAT
- DRIP-DRY
- EASYCLEAN
- MISS CLEANER
- MR. GRANDFATHER'S CLEANER

In an extreme mood you might get this:

- OKAY PLUS

More new names of today:

- FORMULA 405

- REMBRANDT mouthwash

- IMPLANT INNOVATIONS

- GALAXY SCIENTIFIC INC.

## THE TECHNO-TYPE PERSONALITY:

This one is all for Saving the Whale, Saving the Grey Owl, and, for that matter, Saving the Words. This person is inevitably dressed in grunge clothing. You will hear an endless variety of words such as: "MS-DOS." "QWERTY." "RAMROM." "VCRCD." "A.I." "I.S." "CNM." "IMS." "I/O IRDS DPPX."

This type's preferred names include

- nVIEW NETWORK
- dAVID COMPUTERS
- AVRAISYS
- MOUSE INC.
- VR  INC.
- RISKWARE HARDWARE EVERYWHERE

In extremity, you will get such choices as

- VIRTUAL PHOBIA  SYSTEM
- ARTIFICIAL INSANITY CO.

Leading names of the Techno-Types today:

- hDC COMPUTERS INC.
- XTree
- COMPUSA
- IVAX
- EXABYTE
- INTUIT
- IOMEGA

## THE STRATEGIC-TYPE: A COMPOSITE

This type of personality may not actually exist.
However, the interaction of all the above types
may possibly produce this composite.
This person could be any one of the above
characters, and has only one question:
**"Why the hell do we need a name at all?"**

This one's main interest lies in analyzing and
taking over specific brand names in the
marketplace; understanding the competition and
their powerful names inside-out; has a clear
strategy in mind to launch a new-name project;
and wants to know the best possible procedure in
developing a name, rather than doing it oneself.

We have now come to an end of this seemingly-
satiric, but actually quite realistic exercise.

The above analysis--which is only slightly
tongue-in-cheek--may help you to understand the
input you are getting from a group of people who
are undoubtedly experts in their **own** particular
fields of expertise, but when it comes to naming,
are seriously trapped inside a personality which
is inevitably detrimental to this crucially
important exercise.

On many occasions, respective heads of
manufacturing, finance, marketing, advertising,
strategic planning, each place their respective and
respectable heads into a different pile of sand.

If finance could only see things the way that
advertising does!  If manufacturing could only
see the way marketing does. . . .
The multi-disciplinary corporate tension--which
is truly  essential to the company's progress in its
field--now becomes the most detrimental factor
in internal naming at this state of the operation.

And even if your company can survive this stage,
there are all the other serious hurdles to
developing a good name--from gender bias to
political correctness; from foreign languages to
translations; from suitability to availability; and
a dozen more issues with which one must deal.

Names are not developed for the CEO or head
of finance, or engineering VP or the ad geniuses.
They are only for the customers and
shareholders, and have only one function:

To sell the concept in the public's mind.

It ain't easy.

*Please feel free to circulate a
photocopy of this chapter for
your future naming projects.*

# Focus Groupies

**3**

Why doesn't the Old
School of Naming
work anymore?
For that matter,
why don't naming
contests or focus
groups work either?

*ne of the major reasons why so many names fail nowadays, is because most companies still follow the now ancient and justly discredited "Naming School of the '50s." Here are listed its dangerous characteristics, which* ***one must never follow today:***

This is how major international names were created back then:

As a start, companies formed many carefully selected and managed focus groups, lead by a trained psychologist who was skilled in this area. All members of each group were usually from only one nationality, and were specially chosen for their skills with language.

Their task was to develop words, word-roots, analogies, phrases and ideas, in line with chosen themes.

During this 2-to-3 hour session, a group
of six to eight people created up to 500 to 1000
names, words, and roots in total.  Copywriters
would then "build up" from this consumer-based
data an extensive list of potential trademarks--
often as many as 10,000 names, even more.

Computers were also used, to search through
dictionaries; identify names which possessed
"required attributes" (such as manly, exotic,
stylish, etc.); and take existing names.and use
word-splicing techniques to build "new
and more interesting" ones. These thousands of
names would then be pared down to manageable
proportions by eliminating all hard-to-pronounce
words, hard-to-remember ones, those with no
trademark-ability, names where were
too long, etc.

When down to a "preferred short list" of some
20 to 30 names, the lucky winners were checked
in all languages, tested with consumers, and
ranked according to preference.

Consumers were asked to rate the names on
a "like" versus "dislike" basis, only occasionally
noting "male vs. female," "weakness vs.
strength," and so on.  After "legal screening,"
the list was cut down even further; a full legal
search now began, using extensive trademark and
legal staff, admittedly both expensive and time-
consuming.

**Some** type of name was eventually created!

The weakness of this system is clearly obvious to us today.  And that is why, every hour around the clock, a major corporation in North America is **forced** to change its name.

The reasons may vary, from a name no longer conveying what the company does, to similarities and confusions in the marketplace with existing trademarks, or because they are found to be too foreign, or even obscene, in the global marketplace.

If you, or your colleagues, are still following the above methodology, then be careful: **more name changes are just around the corner.**

Let me now show you why naming contests and focus groups fail.

## CONTESTS WHERE EVERYONE LOSES

If you are a parent, do you recall how you named
your child(ren)?  Did you gather together men
and women off the street--making sure you got a
fair selection of sex, visible minority groups, the
physically-challenged, and so forth--and sit them
around a table in your living room until they
came up with the proper name for dearest junior?

Or perhaps you held a contest--just amongst
the members of your family and your spouse's
family, of course--to choose the best possible
name for the latest addition to the clan?
(Even if the winner ended up being "Rambo" or
"PacMan," and the child was a **girl**, a contest **is**
a contest, after all.  Our congratulations to all
who entered.)

I trust that my point is clear:  Corporations are
frequently faced with the challenge of changing
their name, whether because they have broadened
their scope, or become more international, or
whatever.  And it **is** a challenge, as this book
should be clarifying.

Many companies, recognizing the growth of
democracies around the world, and recalling that
key word of the 1980s--**empowerment**--attempt
to be democratic.

## USAGE OF LETTERS OF THE ALPHABET

Approximate
volume of usage
of the letters of the
English alphabet:

13%: **e**
10%: **t**
7%: **o,a,n,i,r,s**
5%: **h**
3%: **d,l,u,c,m,p,f**
2%: **y,w,g,b**
.5%: **v,k,j,x,z,q**

In the newly- freed countries of Eastern Europe, we should all applaud this desire. But there should be no pleasure in witnessing "Company-wide Naming Contests" being joyfully announced, with a very juicy carrot as the grand prize.

Really!! If a global image and a name identity are among the most important issues of business communication today, then why on earth are these companies choosing to run naming contests? One doubted if they would hold a contest to decide who their next C.E.O. would be!

One agonizing example of the above is the story behind UNISYS. The name was eventually launched though a multi-million dollar advertising campaign, simultaneously carried around the globe, while they strangely ignored the fact (well-known to everyone except those who chose the lucky winner) that there were many hundreds of similar and even identical names in dozens of countries! A new cliché might have been born here: "**Democratic** (if not always **great**) minds think alike."

Somehow, this multi-billion-dollar corporation and multi-national company never truly positioned "Unisys," yet, to be fair, the name **has** survived.

And, to be brutally honest, it was a mediocre name, and **remains** a mediocre name within the contents of its identity, standing not-quite tall-enough amongst the other giants of the computer industry.

Not so long ago, another leader in another industry decided that they needed a new name. The company was British Petroleum, and, after a growing awareness of its colonies' loosening ties with the mother country, they decided to hold a contest to decide a new name for its Canadian operation.

And the winner was. . . (the envelope, please): Talisman!

Yes, Talisman was the final choice. The question which some might ask themselves is, "Is Talisman **really** a thoughtful, impressive name for a major corporation?"

Does it carry an image of a small-time flea market operator, or of a place where one can eagerly drive in and cry out "Fill 'er up!" And, you may not be surprised to hear that there are **hundreds** of companies around the world which use the same name: Talisman Crystals. Talisman Lamp Fuels. Talisman Charms.

By the way, the staff employee who thought up the new name for British Petroleum's Canadian operations received 250 shares of the company as a prize.

## SKYDOME

A wide-open contest was held in Canada to chose a name for the soon-to-open domed stadium in Toronto. Some 150,000 entries suggested 12,879 different names. (Note how many must have chosen the exact same one.) The eventual winner was SkyDome-- a name chosen by many hundreds. Two suggestions which were quickly eliminated were Meet-Ball Dome and Hog Dome.

## FEELINGS ABOUT LETTERS

A study of consumer preference for letters of the alphabet discovered that **A, B, S,** and **M** produced the "most favorable feelings" in those interviewed, while **Q, X, Z, F,** and **U** produced the "worst feelings."

So here is a simple new rule to remember: **Running internal naming contests within any organization is not only a time-consuming, frustrating and potentially hostile exercise, but a highly costly one,** producing tedious searches though useless name entries. And what you end up with, almost inevitably, are names such as Unisys and Talisman--words which do not only **not** trip off the tongue, but make one **less** likely to make the trip to the computer store or gas station.

If one wishes to get a sense of the utter ineffectiveness of a naming contest, simply stop 20 people in the corridors or elevators of you office building, and ask them **their** opinions. And forget about the opinions of tens of thousands, as in the sad case of Unisys.

Indeed, Naming Contests are not unlike working with a very large focus group--which leads us to our next concern. . .

## FOCUS GROUPS DON'T WORK

**Focus groups!** Just the sound of the phrase has a magical quality: To be "focused" is to have your head on straight; to have your eye on the main goal; to know precisely what must be done. And "group" radiates with a warm sense of involvement, caring--yes, of **democracy**.

To paraphrase the famous quotation, democracy is a lousy system, but it's still way ahead of anything in second place. Or, to quote directly from a famous essay by the great British writer E.M. Forster, "Two Cheers for Democracy." It's a wonderful system of government.

**But it is no way to choose a name for a company or a product!**

Do focus groups have any value? You bet. They are superb for gathering new research on a concept; for creating interesting, often highly creative ideas; for discovering public opinion about something. But they are **not** for developing names!

To invite ten people off a highway with a coffee/donut/dinner incentive is simply not the correct way to determine what something new should be called. The participants, both confined and obliging (and probably hungry as well), are all longing for human interaction far more then they are interested in solving your problem.

Indeed, They are, more often then not, on the "research circuit " of several different focus group organizations. Focus groupies, if you wish.

Let's picture it for a moment: a group of men and women, who are (in fact) quite **un**focused when first gathered together, who begin to act and pretend, like a jury, in an attempt to pass judgment on a name. Arguments fly. Questions and hands are both raised, and then lowered.

**Is this name capable of killing the competition?**

**Is this name too soft or too macho?**

**Will this name kill the entire venture, or will it make it take off like a rocket?**

Are the discussions, and the decisions, **logical**? Or are they simply part of a process of selecting something in an "eeny, meeny, miney, moe" fashion?

Two hours later, the verdict is in.

The game is over.

**History is about to be made.**

I used the image of a jury just now, but I'd better
backtrack here: This is an amateur approach.
The legal profession calls upon sophisticated and
careful screening of every jury member to
achieve fairness and neutrality.
(Or, at the very least, to try to avoid, as much as
humanly possible, **un**fairness and **pre**-judging.)

Imagine if a major murder trial simply went out
on the street and chose twelve men and women
at random ("eeny, meeny, miney, moe") and
took them into the courtroom to begin
hearing evidence!

Not unlike that sensitive murder trial,
**the selection of a name is an incredibly
sensitive exercise!** Apart from creative,
suitability, availability, and registrability,
the entire question of political correctness is
present. Gender biases. Ethnic slurs and
assumptions. Translations. Profanities.
Racial associations. And much, much more.

Would you invite a Harvard MBA onto a
murder jury? Possibly. Would you ask the same
Harvard MBA to assist you in naming a beer
for the Hispanic market? That would be
high risk, and no different then asking a team
of senior mainframe marketers to come up
with a name of a desktop product. Not only do
the latter lack any exposure to the operation of
a desktop set-up, but they probably even carry
resentment toward the names in the desktop
markets.

Similarly, if your firm desires to sell sugar-free products, you need not necessarily seek out diabetics.

The point is this:  In choosing a new name, whether for a service, consumer product, or a multi-billion-dollar company, **you must look for neutrality, fairness, and absolutely zero personal opinions!**

**Names are not for a group of people!
They are for the masses.**

Thus, to have a gathering of people discuss a naming issue, you must expect long discussions and few viable names to survive the process of elimination.  You must also be prepared to deal with all personalities, and you may have to isolate negative participants.

The problem is, from a purely psychological point of view, one personifies one's own desires and wishes.  So, in a very distorted way-- almost like in a carnival mirror--the outcome of a focus group  on naming is nearly always a deception or a facade.

When asked to express or chose a name, **most** individuals try to assume a strange role, whether it be a follower, or a Power Leader.

Awkwardly, this creates either loose-ends  or a
stalemate, and the result of an unfocused
discussion which does not lend itself to a credible
analysis of the decision at hand.  In other words,
focus groups tend to lead to unfocused, vague,
even dangerous conclusions.

The highly personal opinions of likes and dislikes
which one encounters in most focus groups
sound like a selection match in a dating club.
"Is he a smoker?" and "Will he accept my
children?" have their place, but not in a
focus group dedicated to choosing a name.
Does a name sound Japanese?  Or is it more
Italian?  Is it too artsy?  Maybe too WASPy?

This is not the way to select a name for a product
which could save one company from disaster;
make another company enter the Big Leagues;
make a hundred thousand shareholders want  to
jump for joy, or jump from an office tower.

This is the last decade of the 20th century, when
languages, cultures, global free trades and highly
interactive populations have made the
once-simple question of naming into an all-out
international issue.  To understand these highly
technical matters--including naming trends,
trademark laws, psycho graphics,
psycho linguistics, translations, phonetics,
and more, requires highly specialized input.

It does **not** need, nor will it respond to, a group of men and women called together into a room. Even if there are really fresh donuts for everybody involved.

*In conclusion, do focus groups have value?*

*Of course they do! If you wish to change the graphics of a product. If you wish to do taste tests. Even if you wish to have a "fun exercise" on the names of a competitor.*

*But never forget: Names like Poison, Opium perfume, Xerox, Exxon, even Apple Computers, would have never, ever come out of a focus group exercise.*

*Or even survived one.*

# Naming Business Dreams:  Surnames

4

Using a surname
in business is best
when the founder
is preferably dead.
But why?

 *aming has been going on since the invention of the wheel. And nearly everyone has been confronted with the need to name someone or something, whether a new pet or a new product. The origins of those namings can come in countless ways: from sudden inspiration, by accident, or through stream-of-consciousness thinking while sitting in a traffic jam.*

The world of business, of course, calls for far more logical, thoughtful, creative, and careful consideration in the choosing of a name. Every executive eventually faces the issue of naming a new product, service, venture or even the company itself. And the name of that product, service or company can often make the difference between survival and bankruptcy; between great success and crashing failure.

The average consumer is bombarded by more than 4,000 messages every day, ranging from TV and newspaper ads to electronic billboards.

**The names heard and seen in those various media will reach the public consciousness only if they are unique, distinctive and memorable.**

The question is:  What have been the various sources for company names, and what inspired them?  And how might we learn from these glimpses into the past, to better choose for our own future?

There are all kinds of names--in a wide range of choices--from creative to composed to abstract.

But most names fit into the following four categories:

## MARIO

The heroic plumber named "Mario," known to hundreds of millions of lovers of Nintendo games, received his moniker from the name of the landlord who angrily demanded late rent on that company's warehouse in Seattle, where the game was being developed.

But what if the landlord's name had been Washington or Tyrone?

## SURNAMES:
Using family names as corporate identifiers.

## GEOGRAPHIC NAMES :
Using municipal, regional or other general geographic denominators.

## DESCRIPTIVE/ DICTIONARY NAMES :
Using words from a dictionary, or a descriptive phrase.

## COINED NAMES :
Using composed alphastructures.

These four types of names constitute a very large majority of business names around the world, although there are others, of course. In order to determine these styles, the names have been defined so that they could be indexed and classified for this book.

# FROM ADAM'S GARDEN TO KRAFT'S FOOD--USING A FAMILY NAME FOR CORPORATE IDENTITY

Two centuries ago, nearly every business in North America was named after its founder. The desire to immortalize oneself by putting one's name upon a company or product is undeniable.

Right into the dawn of the 20th century this pattern continued, as American business was dominated by men of passionate, entrepreneurial drive. These men had vision; they had energy; they had innovative and highly original concepts. And they created corporations of often international scope which have become legendary.

And the men who proudly slapped their surnames upon their cars, razors, sewing machines, radios and tires were true visionaries, who often invented their products, or at the very least initiated business concepts and empires, and totally controlled them during their lifetimes.

## PARKER PENS

The slogan used by Parker Pen Company when it created a fountain pen which did not leak: "Avoid embarrassment-- use Parker pens."

The meaning of this slogan to Spanish-speaking consumers in Latin America: "Avoid pregnancy- -use Parker pens."

Let us all congratulate Parker on its break-through discovery in contraceptive research.

**COKE IS IT**

In 1984, a
Vermont man
named Frederick
Karel Koch
(rhymes with
bloke) decided
to change
his name to
"Coke-Is-It,"
after decades of
having his name
mispronounced.

Coca-Cola
promptly filed
an appeal to block
the use of its
trademark.

Is "Frederick Karel
YouGotTheRight
OneBabyUhHuh"
still available?

Their names have become part of the world's vocabulary, and they come quickly and naturally to mind:

HEINZ

FORD

KRAFT

GILLETTE

SINGER

EDISON

FIRESTONE

And many more. These personal, family names eventually become "brand names," and identifying marks of great and admirable businesses.

We have long witnessed how men and women have strived to bring glory and honor to "the family name." (The images of the Kennedy family in the United States--from Joseph's ambassadorship to England during World War II to John Fitzgerald's presidency; from Robert's tragically-aborted run for the same post to Ted's scandal-ridden life and often admirable senatorial career--show how this internal desire remains with us to this day.) But would you bank at First Kennedy & Loan Inc? Perhaps.

Businesses--like political dynasties--have acted in similar fashion: a drive to achieve a desirable reputation and goodwill within the community/country; great effort and expense made to keep that name admired and beyond reproach. In the case of the former, the name would be zealously guarded, to keep others from borrowing or imitating it, and thus risking losing millions of dollars in business which their goodwill--and quality product--had earned. One almost tragic example of not protecting a name is the recent case of Halston.

## THE TRAGEDY OF HALSTON

Halston, the pre-eminent fashion designer in the United States for over a decade, sold his name in 1973 to the Norton Simon Conglomerate, which was then run by a good friend of his. A decade later, Esmark Inc. owned it; in the mid-80s, it moved to Beatrice; then BCI Holdings Corp., and eventually Playtex; in 1986, the Revlon Group bought it.

## IKEA

The name of the billion-dollar furniture company came from Ingvar Kamprad, who was from a family farm called Elmtaryd, which was near the Swedish village of Agunnaryd. When you take the first letters of Mr. Kamprad, his farm, and his village, you end up with a roomful of furniture.

So how about the name IDOMO, their multi-billion dollar competitor?

73

## WENDY'S

Nick-name of the youngest daughter of Dave Thomas, the founder of Wendy's: Wendy

Names of Wendy's two older sisters: Pam and Molly

Sales of the hamburger chain in 1990: $3-billion

See you at Pam's? Let's grab a bite at Molly's?

Nearly every owner of the Halston trademark fought with the great designer over his name, and slashed away at his right to design, and he remains unable to use his name to sell products of his creation in the field of fashion.

Today, the name which once dressed Jacqueline Kennedy and Liza Minelli can now be found on labels of dresses designed by someone else, and sold at J.C. Penny.

GETTING TRUMPED

Less sad, but still underlining the importance of protecting a surname-turned-brandname, is a recent court case involving the famous/infamous Donald Trump.

Ed Zito and Patterson Brooks of Atlanta purchased the rights to a classy kind of glossy business cards from California called "Trump Cards." By 1988, the Georgian entrepreneurs were selling $9-million worth of the cards annually through 600 distributors around the world. When the Trump Organization got wind of "their name" being "used," they first offered the partners a tiny cash settlement; then chose to sue in the courts. The real estate tycoon was later quoted as saying that he **had** to sue, lest "we lose control of our best asset, the Trump name." Whatever your opinions of the outspoken Mr. Trump, that quotation should live forever. One's name is, indeed, one's best asset.

## TO SURNAMES WITH LOVE

Right up to today, we see tens of millions of dollars spent annually, advertising a good family/brand name, keeping it ever-present in the minds of the public, and maintaining its sense of "leadership" among the countless competitors in the ever-more-crowded marketplace. The "interesting" surnames which have become famous as highly successful, internationally admired products, are legion:

> BALLY
> BATA
> BOEING
> CINZANO
> COLGATE
> PORSCHE

## BUILDING BLOCHS

When Henry Bloch created his tax-preparing firm, H & R Block, he intentionally changed the spelling, so that people would not be confused with two possible pronounciations and spellings of his name. But as time went on, and he appeared on television as president of H & R Block, his name appeared as "Bloch," and caused serious corporate communication confusion, due to the different spellings and pronounciation. Finally, to simplify it, he eventually adopted his company's name as his own: Henry Block.

## HUMOROUS ACRONYMS

An editorial in **Advertising Age:**

Last week we reported that **S&S** sold its stock in **WPP,** which recently acquired **JWT,** to avoid the wrath of **P&G,** which wanted some action **PDQ.** This followed **S&S'** move to join **B&S** with Bates to form **BSBW.** Also, last week **Y&R** combined **DYR** and **HCM,** in order to more successfully compete with **BBDO, O&M, FCB, DMB&B, BJK&E,** et al.

Who's running this business, Vanna White?

Ralph Lifshitz, a young New York designer, chose to change unpleasant-sounding name to RALPH LAUREN, which is now a multi-billion dollar clothing enterprise.

Pietro Cardino, of France, took on the name PIERRE CARDIN. This French-sounding name is the largest apparel exporter in that country.

Over the past few decades, we have seen many other surnames undergo modifications similar to that of Mr. Marcel Bich, and then used as the names of the products they manufacture.
A Japanese firm called Konishiroku produces cameras which have been named Konica.
A formula for antiseptics by Sir Joseph Lister is still used in a product called Listerine.
John Rawlings invented a plug which he christened Rawlplug.

Charles Revson's company chose to adapt his surname to "Revlon," and even used his given name in a line of products labeled "Charlie."

Surnames have long been used--with varying degrees of success--in naming both companies and the products they manufacture, and they probably always will.

The descendants of those early geniuses of American entrepreneurship **rarely** run their "family" businesses nowadays. Indeed, today's international corporations and conglomerates are more often managed by Harvard MBAs and other hired, non-related guns.

Furthermore, mergers and acquisitions have proven to be effective and efficient means of growth for hundreds of firms, making it unlikely that any one individual can hold public attention and company control in the same powerful manner, and for any length of time, as the Fords, Morgans and Mellons once had the inspiration and ability to do.

Just as the majority of major companies are more often managed by professional "teams" than by popular individuals, we have seen ongoing, broad-based commercialization becoming far more favored than the promotion of any one individual.

In the closing decades of this century, we **rarely** encounter a massive commercial entity, created single-handedly by a larger-than-life personality, bearing the surname of its proud, vain founder.

Examples of this latter truth abound:
Corporate names such as APPLE and MICROSOFT fill our minds and offices, and not

JOBS COMPUTERS INC. or

GATES SOFTWARE UNLIMITED.

Nor do we see the name CROC HAMBURGERS slashed across the front of ten thousand stores around the world; it is McDONALD'S which is emblazoned instead.

**KARL MARX UNIVERSITY**

The Karl Marx University of Economics of Hungary recently changed its name to the Budapest School of Economics.

Can you blame them?

77

## FAMILIES HAVE PROBLEMS, TOO

Indeed, **potential liabilities** have arisen over the years, in those cases where a dynamic founder's surname continues on a company's letterhead and products.  First, as noted with the Kennedy dynasty in the U.S., both the founder and his family **must** avoid scandal and public embarrassment which could cause damage to its name.  The pro-Hitler stance taken by Henry Ford for many years, along with his involvement in virulent anti-Semitic publications and pronouncements, tainted that excellent company and its fine automobiles for many decades.

And how about the De Lorean Corp., maker of the gull-winged stainless steel car?  The founder was caught up in an ugly drug bust, which cast horrible shadows across his highly-creative concept for automobiles.  He was not even able to sell his company after the incident.

For that matter, how about the once attractively-named Helmsley Palace of Manhattan?  The opening  paragraph of a front page story in **The New York Times** business section on November 1, 1993, says it all:  "The royal family of Brunei has agreed to buy the New York Palace Hotel on Madison Avenue for $202 million.  The luxurious 54-story hotel's previous name, the Helmsley Palace, became a major liability when Leona Helmsley was sentenced to prison in 1989 for tax evasion and mail fraud."

And further problems:  When a founder dies,
or any of his immediate heirs do the same, public
confidence in a company can be severely shaken.
Recall the drop in Ford Motor Company
share prices when old Henry finally
drove to meet his maker.

Confusion can also be caused when a founder
becomes estranged from his/her company, as
with Dr. Cray and Cray Research.

And even an **orderly** succession of management
power from father to son--Wang Computer is
one sad example--can unsettle both investors
and customers alike--often with very good
reason.

Most recently, we have seen the crumbling
of several real estate empires, ranging from
the Reichmann family's Olympia & York to
those of Robert Campeau and Donald Trump--
the latter two with their names prominently
displayed upon their stocks and their office
towers.  When Campeau took over the Federal
and Allied retail empires--leading to disastrous
personal and corporate financial difficulties--
the danger of using one's surname became
horrifyingly clear:

Utilizing one's name as a corporate identity might
impress mom, or drive an older brother into fits
of jealousy, but can make one doubly vulnerable
when things go badly.

When the city of Toronto, Canada was struggling over a name for its new domed stadium, then being built in 1985, I was interviewed about the possibility of naming it after a prominent politician.

I reminded the reporters of the dumping of a number of Canadian political leaders by the public, soon after they had been held in great respect and popularity.

"Imagine if a stadium had been named after **them?**" I warned. (It was eventually labelled SkyDome--a name produced by a widely-entered contest--but one which was **still** eventually legally-challenged in the courts.)

## A BULL IN A CHINA SHOP

It is common to find major companies struggling
with names which have numerous trademark
problems, and several studies which show that
their name is not working.  And on top of all
these international problems, they find countries
where the name is obscene!

Why?

Most often, leadership simply lacks the guts--
from lower management up to the CEO--
to come out and say: "The Emperor Has
No Clothes."  Or No Name, for that matter.

A quarter-century ago, when I used to sell
Honeywell Computers in Montreal,  the makers
of the products were a proud, $2-billion
company.  At the same time, IBM was a
$7-billion company.  Today, Honeywell sells
**less than $2-billion a year.**  And IBM, despite
its well-known problems, losses, and cutbacks in
personnel, remains a world-wide leader, with
**over $65-billion** in sales.

I use this example for good reason.  For the past
15 years, at least, Honeywell has had to struggle
for its very identity, going through at least five
full-blown and costly advertising campaigns, and
the new name "BULL"--a highly-respected
family name in Europe.

Because of the image of a "bull market" on Wall Street, the use of the name "bull" in any **other** context creates real problems. True, Bull is the widely-respected surname of an admired French family with quality experience in communications, and the largest shareholders in Honeywell, but it remains an unacceptable name, internationally.

Nearly a decade ago, I was actually told by their committee that "our first choice is to look for a new name; our second choice is Bull." As you already know, the leaders of Honeywell were unable to find an intelligible name, and thus were forced to go with their second choice.

Yes, this was another typical failure of both focus groups and internal naming.

A few years later, I was called by Honeywell once again, which now had a joint venture with Texaco in process management. I ended up naming the new business **ICOTRON** for them. Meanwhile, they had spent millions upon millions of dollars to play on words such as "GLO-BULL." It simply did not work.

Other examples abound: DAIWOO has had an endless struggle with constantly advertising "YOU KNOW WHO--DAIWOO"--yet it continues to find itself anonymous, after countless dollars miserably wasted on advertising.

**And the beat goes on. . . .**

In the late 1980s, ABC Namebank undertook
a major study to assess the role of corporate
naming in North America.  In order to measure
the changing nature of corporate naming, we
used **Fortune 500** as the source.

In 1955, the first listing of **Fortune 500**
companies was published.  For this study,
we took a year-by-year comparative analysis
over a 30 year period, to demonstrate distinct
patterns and the rise and fall in the types of
corporate names.

From the time that **Fortune** magazine published
its first listing of the top 500 industrials in
America, down to today, one can see a distinct
pattern of the lessening of the use of surnames
in the names of corporations:

## SURNAMES

1955                                                    1992

215                                                     185

The problems in using a surname from a powerful, inspirational, entrepreneurial founder in one's business, are most evident:
They are declining in use, over the years.

Any **personal** liabilities of the founder and/or his descendants and family, are perceived as **corporate** ones.

These names are rarely geared to a rapidly-changing, often global, business environment.

The absence of a founder, or his death, can create uncertainty, confusion, and even loss of faith in the company, its products and services.

*As we have seen, using a family name in business can be manageable, while the bearer of the name is still alive and ticking.*

*Otherwise--be careful.*

# Naming Business Dreams:  Geographic Names

5

Names from the atlas
can keep you
surprisingly local:
The demise of
geographic names

 *ames of villages, towns, cities and regions eventually create territorial limitations for businesses. With the inevitable global free trade, the **origin** of a product will become less important than ever.*

This category includes the multitude of companies which chose to use geographic denominators as part of their names. Not surprisingly, territorial names flourished over the years, as American business grew. Not unlike the surnames of the Edison and the Goodyear companies, many firms which began in various towns, regions and states wished to proudly declare their birthplaces within their very name.

This often manifested itself in strong trends. A half-century ago, it became highly popular to incorporate the word "American" into a company name--and why not? It made it an almost patriotic act to purchase their product. (And almost "un-American" **not** to do so!)

Thus, the birth of:

- AMERICAN BRANDS
- AMERICAN PAPER
- AMERICAN CYANAMID
- AMERICAN HOME

As once-regional companies slowly grew into powerful national and even international corporations, once-local geography turned into prominent brand names:

- CORNING GLASS
- BURLING CARPETS
- BELL SOUTH
- MID-AMERICAN WASTE SYSTEM

And countless more. Interestingly, many people today automatically associate the word "Corning" with "Corningware," and are not even aware that this was the name of the city where the factory and offices of the Corning Glass Works are located. The same goes for Pontiac, Michigan, which yields its name for a car, even though the name, of course, has far more ancient, historical roots. Oneida, for example, of stainless steel frame, comes from Oneida, New York. Obviously, most place names have histories of their own. But when a town or city becomes a birthplace and namesake of a new product, that product is considered to be named for the place rather than for the person or event which gave that place its name.

## STRANGE, UNKNOWN VILLAGES

True, many have used obscure place names with
great success, such as the Japanese coastal city of
HITACHI; and Shibaura, a region in Japan where
the **To**kyo **Shiba**ura Electronic Company
operated--and which gave the world the now
famous brand name of TOSHIBA.

West Germany's Hoechst, home of
HOECHST CELANESE, took out a double-
paged, word-filled ad recently which declared:

"Our name may be hard to say, but the $1-billion
we spend or research and development speaks for
itself."

I agree.  "One billion dollars" is a **lot** easier
to pronounce than "Hoechst Celanese."

There are problems, too, with geographic names,
the first of which is the most obvious:
**The geographic-hook can imply a geographic
limitation.**  For instance, Eastern Airlines
evolved its name from the simple fact that it
originally concentrated on serving
eastern routes--and **only** eastern routes.
One can see how limiting that name became,
once the company (literally) spread its wings!

Federal Express is similarly troublesome. While the name was **initially** effective in conveying the image of a geographically-positioned, nation-wide courier service, when the firm began to expand **internationally,** the name became far less successful--and far more "limiting." Indeed, it was a result of this fact that Federal Express acquired Flying Tigers, to help create a more global image.

When Canada edged into Free Trade with the United States in the late 1980s, I was interviewed often about how its brand names might fare with its friendly neighbor to the South. I noted that far too many Canadian corporations carried geographic names such as "Canadian," "Northern" and "Arctic," which suggested limitations. There were problems, as well, with names which were linked too closely to Canada-only imagery, such as 2,900 firms with "Royal" in their names, to the 2,100 "Dominions," 1,400 "Imperials," and 1,100 "Crowns." And then there are the even **more** geographically-limiting monikers of the Canadian National Railways, Oshawa Group, and Hudson Bay.

Indeed, names with "north," "northern," "arctic," and even the impressive-sounding "CANADA" **could** alienate American consumers, suggesting coldness and frigidity. (Of course, suggestions of northern-ness and Canadian-origin in ice skates, hockey equipment, winter wear, beer and snow tires could provide an advantage, yes?)

**MINOLTA**

An acronym derived from **M**achine, **IN**strument, **O**ptica**L** and **TA**jima, the latter being the name of a Japanese wholesale firm (Tajima Shoten) run by the father of the founder of MINOLTA Camera Co.

89

## LUBRICATING COMPANY NAMES

Most names of oil and gas exploration companies refer to their place of origin, of course, such as Standard Oil of New Jersey, Texaco, First Calgary Petroleums Ltd.; or to their founders.

**VICKS/WICKS**

When Vicks cough drops entered the German marketplace, it was stunned to discover that "vicks" is slang in that language for sexual intercourse.

The company quickly changed its name to Wicks in that market.

But there are times when one has to stifle the giggles, if not the investment:

- COURAGEOUS EXPLORATION INC.
- PANACHE PETROLEUM INC.
- PANHANDLE EASTERN
- WALKING  STICK OIL & GAS LTD.
- FORTUNE PETROLEUM LTD.
- GREYPOWER RESOURCES
(you guessed it; this one was founded by a group of semi-retired men)

And, for those of you who just love to buy penny stocks on the always dangerous Vancouver Stock Exchange:

- LAST DITCH INVESTMENTS INC.

**Good luck!**

# C A S E   S T U D Y :

## COINING A NAME TO ESCAPE GEOGRAPHY

In 1905, Colonel McCormick, the founder of **The Chicago Tribune**, ventured north into the infinite wilderness of Ontario, and set up a newsprint operation on a large acreage on the banks of the Welland Canal. The company was called Ontario Paper Company, which eventually became Quebec & Ontario Paper Company, and is still owned by the famous Tribune Company of Chicago. Its head office is located at the ultra-modern newsprint plant on the outskirts of St. Catherines, Niagara Falls.

This nearly-century old historic corporate landmark, in the provinces of Ontario and Quebec, is perhaps, surprisingly, the 7th largest newsprint maker in all of North America. In the early 90s, it faced its classic problem, frequently discussed in this book: It wanted to shed its geographic limitation.

The company was extremely proud of its illustrious and ancient history, and its rich evolution as a major newsprint supplier.

When I met their CEO and their Naming Committee, they had already gone through several internal attempts over the previous years. They had yet to come up with a satisfactory solution.

And they needed a highly creative solution, too. In order to satisfy both its workers and its executives, they had to incorporate their peculiar geography and the bi-lingual nature of their employees in their new name.

At the same time, they wished to become a world-class player in the paper business, and shed the old image of "only" newsprint, logging, and regional image.

The task, from the outset, was exceedingly sensitive: They were locked into geography, yet they wanted a new metamorphosis, and initial public share offering for sale on the stock market.

In my presentations, attended by legal, marketing, manufacturing, management people, others from public affairs, advertising, financial, the CEO, and Tribune management, I developed the name **QUNO**. The transition went smoothly and successfully.

And today, a few years after, it retains, in a subtle way, both original place names of Quebec and Ontario. Furthermore, it is an internationally transparent name, legally secured, and has been well-received by both the industry and in the world at large.

## BANKING ON NAMES

Perhaps surprisingly, financial institutions have
been changing their names faster in the
United States than any other corporate group.
In the first six months of 1991, for example,
148 banks and other financial firms changed
names, which was 32% of the 462 major name
changes, much higher than the second largest
category (manufacturing firms), of which
26% made that major move.

Some stories of bank name changes are highly
instructive, if not particularly happy ones.
One of the major banks to cast off its geographic
identify in the area of Washington, D.C. was
the newly-merged Virginia National Bank and
First & Merchants National Bank, in 1983.

Then, in 1986, D.C. National Bank and
Suburban Bancorp of Bethesda, Maryland,
joined the family.  A new name was chosen--
Sovran Financial Corp.--and a $2.7-million
advertising campaign helped to gain the new
name acceptance in the lucrative market of the
nation's capital.

But then, in 1989, Sovran merged with
Citizens and Southern Corp., moving the now-
accepted Sovran to become "Avantor."  The joke
around the Washington area was that it sounded
more like a European car than an American bank,
and "Avantor" went by the wayside, as well.

Briefly, C&S/Sovran was on their letterheads, until it chose **another** new name, "NATIONSBANK," to let everyone know just how national, yet international, this financial institution was.
Whew.

Some bank names, of course, would **never** be chosen today, such as Morgan, Chemical, and Citibank, but the long history of each has given them clout and respect.  Still, this professional namer doubts if "Chemical" will survive as a name, if only because of the growth of the environmental movement, and the awareness that many chemicals can be dangerous to humans, whether on our bodies or inside them.

**ChemPlus** has been introduced as a service to the valued customers of the Chemical Bank, with millions of posters and billboards all over America.   An alchemist's dream!

Bank names, then, are like the names which all other companies which chose to do business internationally:  They should be credible, globally clear, distinct, powerful, memorable, linguistically sound, and transcultural.

So, when BankAmerica and Security Pacific chose to merge in the summer of 1991, they chose BankAmerica--leaving no doubt as to its major, international standing.

At the turn of the century, banks were built solidly like funeral homes, and their names were created to reflect solidity and strength.

By mid-century, mass marketing and mass appeal demanded flexibility and reliability in names, and we now take that for granted. But as the millennium approaches, the emphasis has been on personalization, intelligence, environmental consciousness, and life enhancement.

## NAMING LANDS

When Columbus first set foot on the New World, he never imagined he would lose out to Amerigo Vespucci, a navigator who had a better sense of marketing his name than Chris.

But how about the giant land mass to the north? In 1867, the fathers of the about-to-be-founded new country struggled with each of the following names, before correctly choosing "Canada":

--LAURENTIA
--NEW BRITAIN
--CABOTIA
--COLUMBIA
--BORETTA
--BRITANNICA
--URSALIA
--MESOPALAGIA
--KINGDOM OF
  CANADA

# CASE STUDY:

## FROM WESTERN CANADA TO THE ENTIRE WORLD

In the fall of '93, Bell Atlantic announced its merger with TCI, creating one of the largest telecommunications conglomerates of our time. This merger alone puts the company on a global map which far transcends that very limiting name of "Atlantic."

Out in the Western Canadian province of Alberta was an 80-year-old telephone company called, understandably, Alberta Government Telephone.

It was the largest single employer in that province (after the government itself), and its multi-billion-dollar sales placed it among the top ten phone companies in North America.

A few years ago, this major public institution decided to privatize, which led to three immediate problems regarding its name:
It was no longer a government body;
it would no longer serve **only** the province of Alberta, since it planned to go internationally;
and it was no longer only a telephone company, but would now handle all emerging telecommunication services.

When I was called to the boardroom situated
on the top floor of the largest office tower in
Calgary, I was given no easy mandate and task:
to find a name which would be acceptable to
its customer base (then, all of the taxpayers of
Alberta), yet somehow reflect, predict and
suggest its future growth.

And more:  I had to also find a new moniker
which would be acceptable to its board;
to the Alberta government and its politicians
(since they were still a considerable player);
and to consumers around the globe, where it
would be bidding aggressively as an emerging
international telecommunications player.

Naturally, it was hoped that any new name would
be good for ticker-tapes; on the stock market;
as a sponsor of football and other sporting
events; in advertisements; on T-shirts and coffee
mugs and even the uniforms of its repair-persons.
And 'COKE' was already taken!

In order to address this major concern, we had
to step back and analyze the situation:  With
the break-up of AT&T, not only some two dozen
Baby Bells had come about, all of them with
names which had a ring to them:

- BELL SOUTH
- BELL ATLANTIC
- CINCINNATI BELL
- BELL CANADA

Then there were:

- NYNEX
- PACTEL
- USWEST.

Then there was also the invention and rise of the
cellular phone; the deregulation of hardware;
the coming of the fax machine:  These had
created several thousands of new telephone-
service names!  And in North America alone,
this was compounded by several **million**
new hi-tech company names, as well.

Our challenge was to find a name that, on
immediate aural or visual contact, would
somehow spell out TELEPHONE.
That, and not sound like a petroleum jelly
company or a baby food manufacturer,
or a real estate operation, or a toy company!

We **had** to make sure that the new name
sounded clearly as if it represented a full-blown,
full-service telecommunication company,
with all the many service which that now
suggests and provides.

Naturally, there had been the dilution of such
names as "Bell,"  "Alex," and countless others.
And we could clearly **not** touch "PHONE," in
spite of our need to imply it.

When we prepared our research, we found that there were two major "keys" to what we wished to express in this name:

- TELECOMMUNICATIONS
- UNIVERSALITY.

And so we developed "**TELUS**." It was quickly registered in 80 countries around the world, and launched with great hoopla. And I am pleased to report that it is a **very** successful name in world telecommunications today. Indeed, we have subsequently been invited to name several other projects for TELUS, which we have done-- with the satisfaction and speed of a good fax or cellular call.

## GEOGRAPHIC NAMES ARE RAPIDLY DROPPING OFF THE MAP

From the previous examples, we have seen the clear demise of the geographic name.  Indeed, of all the many different types of corporate names in existence today, it is those with geographic connotations which are most rapidly being eliminated.  After all, firms which were once-powerful regional leaders have now become competitors on the international scene.  A global economy makes it increasingly apparent that old images of local territories are potential liabilities for companies which are expanding internationally.

Once again, the **Fortune 500** shows a diminishing pattern of these kind of corporate names:  And through the next few years, this number will undoubtedly continue to decline dramatically.

## GEOGRAPHIC NAMES

| 1955 | 1992 |
|------|------|

| 82 | 52 |
|----|----|

The problems, then, with geographic names, are
clear.  They are, like the others noted above,
declining rapidly in use.

They inevitably limit the scope of a business,
by implying geographic limitations.

They can create confusion, due to limited
geographic knowledge on the part of consumers.

They are hard to transfer across borders.

They are difficult to move transglobally.

Geographic denominators are often indistinct and
non-proprietary, such as names which use
NATIONAL and WESTERN in them.

*As we have seen, using an atlas
is a wonderful way to find out
where you are.  It's rarely a wise
place to search for a business
name.*

# Naming Business Dreams:
# Descriptive and/or Dictionary Names

6

Describing what
your business does
in an advertisement
is fine; describing it
within the name can
be deadly.

 *hen surnames and geographic names did not provide a sizzle, names were often borrowed from the dictionary to create a modern image. Many companies attempted to ensure a quick visual/auditory association between their corporate name and the industry in which they were thriving.*

And so we saw a category of names which included the applying of dictionary meanings to help identify a company or a product, as well as the use of descriptive phrases as monikers.

This was an understandable desire, considering the times; most businesses in America were still in their early, evolutionary stage.

This trend led to the search for the words to suggest both the dynamic nature of the company, and the generality of its operations.

This is why so many companies ended up with words like "dynamic" and "general" in their names.

Today, every telephone book in every city around the globe still has several pages with almost identical lookalike and soundalike names:

- GENERAL DYNAMICS
- GENERAL MOTORS
- GENERAL ELECTRIC
- GENERAL FOODS
- GENERAL AVIATION
- GENERAL CINEMA
- GENERAL HOMES
- GENERAL HOST
- GENERAL MILLS
- GENERAL NUTRITION
- GENERAL PHYSICS
- GENERAL PUBLIC
- GENERAL SIGNAL

HELP, GENERAL SCHWARZKOPF!!

There was another prevalent trend which reached its peak from the late '30s right though the 1950s: Companies longed to project a national, or international, image, right in their very names.

This led to countless corporate names which were long and very descriptive:

- INTERNATIONAL BUSINESS MACHINES

- INTERNATIONAL CORRESPONDENCE SCHOOL

- INTERNATIONAL PAPER CORPORATION

- INTERNATIONAL TECHNOLOGY CORPORATION

- RADIO CORPORATION OF AMERICA

- THE COUNTRY'S BEST YOGURT,

- I CAN'T BELIEVE IT'S YOGURT,

- THANK GOD IT'S FRIDAY

and so on.

The objective behind these lengthy and mouth-
filling names was a valid one:  A long name
seemed to suggest bigness, and the hint of a giant
company implied both credibility and stability to
the general public.

As times changed and the economy tightened,
these lengthy names began to pose problems
for both companies and customers alike.
For one thing, in a world moving much faster,
complex names took too long to pronounce.
They were difficult to communicate
electronically.

And, to be blunt, they proved inconvenient
on the stock exchange boards.

## HONEYLEMON

In 1989, thirteen different companies in Japan came out with a honey and lemon drink.

**Six** of the firms used the same brand name: HONEYLEMON.

Furthermore, America's industrial boom steadily evolved into a more diversified expansion, through the emergence of both service and finance sectors. In the old days, long names were printed out, letter by giant letter, across the sides of the entire length of several flat buildings, giving drivers monolithic backdrops between trees and forests. The long, single-story industrial building of old gave way to corporate headquarters within urban skyscrapers, creating new space, administration, human resource and image requirements. The older, block-long buildings easily accommodated long names in towering letters, but the high-rise office towers had limited sign space. In addition, long names reduced visibility.

When a Concorde or a 747 descends over the glittering city of New York or Paris, and lands at Kennedy or De Gaulle, the passengers are awed by the handful of bright, shiny, legendary names on the top of the skyscrapers.

By the 1960s, most companies began to shorten, or initialize, their names--"telescoping" them, in other words. "Texas Oil" became TEXACO.

International Business Machines, of course, turned electronically into IBM.
Radio Corporation of America is now RCA.
Minnesota Mining and Manufacturing evolved into 3M. Pepsi-Cola became PEPSICO.

Telescoping went beyond the mere use of once-long company names; it also was reflected in the growing use of acronyms, such as LASER, NASA and RADAR. These were perceived as effective, and often constituted the full name of a corporation, even if they did not always convey any particular sense, or suggestion. Furthermore, it did not take too many years for the available initial combinations to begin to run out.

Today, corporate name Initialization or Telescoping is rarely seen.

Another approach to the creation of names has been to use already-familiar words from the dictionary which have little or no relation to the product being named.

CARNATION, for instance, has been used for both cigars and milk. APPLE, on the other hand, although not associated in any "natural" or "logical" way with computers, has survived as a pure accident.

The names of constellations, zodiac symbols, gemstones, flowers, animals, and everyday items have all been used to name both products and even companies.

The problem is: If the association between object and product is **too** remote, it may be difficult for the consumer to relate the name to the product, or to remember it at all, when it comes time to make a purchase in a store.

## TICKER SYMBOLS

Creative ticker symbols on the NYSE:

COATED SALES INC:
symbol : **RAGS**

ANIMED
symbol: **VETS**

UNITED STOCKYARDS:
symbol: **COW**

CONDATA NEW YORK:
symbol: **CASH**

COOPERVISION
symbol: **EYE**

GENERAL EMPLOYMENT ENTERPRISES
symbol: **JOB**

Many detergents, for example, have been given simple, natural names, which make the buyer think of rushing water:

- TIDE
- SURF
- CASCADE

are three which come easily to mind. These all reinforce the idea of "washing" in the mind of the customer.

Other products have been named for human qualities or emotions, such as

- CHEER
- JOY
- PLEDGE
- PROMISE

To convey images of purity, wholesomeness and honesty, Henry D. Seymour chose the image of the Quaker for his oatmeal cereal. It clearly worked, as anyone can see from the smiling face on the old-fashioned Quaker Oats package on a hundred thousand store shelves.

## WASTING NAMES

Imagine if every garbage bag you threw out over a ten year period was handled by a multi-billion dollar global giant.

Of course, when a firm like that changes a once-descriptive name to a non-descriptive one, there can be major difficulties.

In 1993, Waste Management Inc., the world's leading collector of waste products, changed its name to its stock ticker symbol (and a bit more) , WMX TECHNOLOGIES INC.

And this was a full decade **since** most corporations had begun to drop initials. So, even though the company includes a whole slew of other firms--

Waste Management of North America, consisting of four companies and 30,000 employees;

Chemical Waste Management, Inc., with 4,600 workers;

Rust International Inc., with 12,000 environmental engineers;

Weelabrator Technologies Inc., with 4,000 employees working in environmental services;

## UPS AND DOWNS OF NAMES

Percent of **decrease** in the use of certain words in trademark applications for food and beverages in 1990-1991:

40%: **HEART**
23%: **PURE**
18%: **FRESH**
18%: **MAXI**
18%: **MAX**
14%: **SUPER**

Percent of **increase** in use of certain words in trademark applications for food and beverages in 1990-1991:

25%: **LIGHT**
25%: **LITE**
25%: **NATURE**
25%: **NATURAL**
21%: **ULTRA**
21%: **ENVI-**
17%: **QUALITY**
12%: **VALUE**
10%: **ECHO**

Waste Management International
14,800 workers in foreign countries ;

WMX Technology and Services, providing
corporate support services--one assumes
that the firm will go on being called
"Waste Management" by everyone
who knew it before the change.

True, U.S. Steel became USX Corp., and
American Airlines and United Airlines turned
magically into AMR Corp. and UAL Corp.--
but we all know what those companies are **still**
called by the general public, don't we?

## CASE STUDY:

## GETTING THE MAXIMUM OUT OF A DICTIONARY NAME

A few years ago, we were called by the then-recipient of the International Agency of the Year award, the widely-respected advertising firm of Baker Lovick-BBDO. They had experienced serious difficulties in getting a handle on a name for the largest oil and gas retailer in Canada-- a company with over 4,000 gas stations from coast to coast.

Very quickly, we were able to establish a clear understanding on how to approach a name, and we created a brand name called **MAXIMUM**. It was soon backed by a massive signage on gas stations everywhere, and the public readily bought it. It actually increased the company's marketshare, and made the firm--PetroCanada-- more successful than it had ever been. And, interestingly, it moved many **other** North American oil companies to come up with similar strategies.

While this might look simple at first glance, the difficulties, especially in a country like Canada, was phenomenal. First of all, we must recall that Canada, the second largest country on earth after Russia (yes, it is even larger than China), is officially bi-lingual throughout. This promptly demanded a name which could interact as a real consumer name in both of those tongues.

Certain names, furthermore, can be misleading,
or may upset regulatory bodies over the selling of
gasoline products under false pretenses:
Words such as "high-calibre," for example.

And, as anyone who reads, much less drives,
is quite aware, words like GOLD, SILVER, and
PREMIUM are all used, over-used, and highly
diluted, not only in the oil industry, but all over.

Furthermore, words like PERFORMANCE and
CALIBRE have different meanings and different
connotations to different people, especially those
who speak two quite different languages!

Thus, the complexity of the problem:
A new name needed to be understood by the
entire population, in both its essence, and in
oth languages. It had to give a clear message
which would be accepted by both. That is why
when a car named Vigor came to the market, it
had failed to convey its true essence.

As I developed the name MAXIMUM, there
was a bonus which may **not** be immediately
apparent to most: the word "maximum"
is used on many millions of speed signs in
North America, which creates a reinforcement of
the name, 24-hours-a-day, whenever someone is
on the road, whether walking, biking, or driving.

And so, in all modesty, I believe that the oil
company has gotten the "maximum" value from
its new name--pun intended.

## IN CONCLUSION. . . .

Interestingly, the use of descriptive and/or
dictionary names have **also** tumbled over the
years, as can be seen in comparing the number of
Top 500 corporations bearing these monikers
between **Fortune's** initial listing in 1955, and
today.

## DESCRIPTIVE

1955                                      1992

169                                      124

Here, too, an analysis of descriptive/dictionary
types of names leads to rather negative
interpretations regarding their use today:

These names, like those of family/founder
surnames, are declining steadily in use by
corporations.

These names can be neutralized easily, when the company has any change in the focus of its business. (Today's UNION CARBIDE has very little to do with carbides, does it?)

These names are often cumbersome and awkward.

Often times, the prefix on these kinds of names can be indistinct and, even worse, non-proprietary (such as those with GENERAL and ROYAL in them).

*The dictionary is filled with millions of words and their full meanings. But in business names, full meanings are not essential.*

# Naming Business Dreams:  Coined Names

7

Dancing through the
alphabet, in search of
a meaningful, brief
new word to serve
as a name, is not as
easy as it sounds.

*t is important to know that creating unique alpha-structures is perhaps the most difficult type of name development. This challenge requires sophisticated understanding of global naming trends, languages, psychographics and trademark registerability. By no means is this a game for the Scrabble player, or a focus groupie's pet project. Yet, in the 1970s and since, there has arisen a prevalent practice to use coined names.*

This followed several other trends in naming: The initial/acronym fad, and then a tendency to use two-word names, usually consisting of a strong, powerful word like, Dynamics or Control and a business-related term which did **not** specify any particular type of enterprise or product.

However, when the business dictionaries had been totally ransacked, descriptive names became far more difficult to formulate.

And so, the rise of coined words: Names which were composed through fabrication, telescoping, and many other techniques.

Many coined words such as KODAK , EXXON and XEROX had memorable sounds, but lacked any specific meaning. Powerful-sounding phonetics, such as the letters "X" and "K" were highly-favored, but here, too, the sources quickly dried up, and companies soon turned to softer, less dynamic-sounding consonants.

AN HISTORICAL LOOK AT LINGUISTICS

English is now the most popular language of study outside of English-speaking countries worldwide. But phonetically, it is not an easy language for people of the Far East, because of difficulties in pronunciation of various letters-- R and L being the most notable. This would be an important concern in coining a name for global use.

And there are many more: The Spanish alphabet has no letter W. Italian has no J, K, W, X or Y. Still, English has all the necessary components to produce the business and consumer sounds acceptable on a global scale.

There is now, however, a shifting pattern affecting the use of English components.

## YOUR FINGERS NEEDN'T WALK TOO FAR

In New York City, and for that matter, everywhere else, there are companies such as **A LOCKSMITH** and **AAAAAdirondack Rents** --both created in order to get in the very front of Yellow Pages listings.

If you disagree, or want to take legal action on this stupidity, then you will conveniently find the following firm leading the list in 1993's **Toronto Yellow Pages** under "Lawyers": **AAAAActionLaw.**

Some 20 years ago, most products exported to the American market by Japanese and Far East manufacturers had clear, distinct, English-sounding names such as Sony, Sharp and Panasonic. As innovations in both product development and manufacturing made these name brands synonymous with quality in most international markets, marketers began to seek Japanese or Far Eastern sounds for electronic consumer products.

For example, ATARI, an American company, was creatively named to convey Japanese advanced technology quality in the minds of video game customers. As a result, Korean and Taiwanese manufacturers such as C. Itoh, Miata, Samsung, Hyundi and Fujitsu are all comfortable promoting foreign-sounding non-English names in America and other English-speaking markets.

Phonetically speaking, as we approach the year 2000, the sharp influx of Far Eastern names on the global scene will continue to make naming ever more complex.

Then there are **cultural** obstacles in the launch of corporate product and service names. "Nay" is "yes" to Greeks. The American "yeah" means "no" to Japanese. To the British, phoning long distance is a "trunk" call, a "sister" is a nurse, and "cereal" is cooked porridge and not cold flakes out of a box.

A simple laugh, "Ha, Ha, Ha," means "mother" in Japanese, while "Ohio" is "good morning." In Russian, "look" means "opinion" and "socks" is "juice." In France, a simple sign of "sale" conveys a meaning of "dirty." The Chinese word "mai" said with a certain vocal intonation means "buy" and in another manner means "sell"; when enunciated together, "mai" and "mai" means "business."

To understand the parameters of this language problem, we must consider that there are approximately **2,700 languages with up to 8,000 dialects around the globe.** The key languages are divided into 12 important families with 50 lesser ones. Indo-European is the largest family, in which English is now the most important category.

## STICKY VALDEZ

In 1990, the Exxon **Valdez**--the tanker which caused the worst oil spill in the history of North America--changed its name to the Exxon **Mediterranean,** reflecting its new area of deployment.

Wouldn't **you** want to change your name after destroying a large area of Alaska?

Based on usage by population, here is a list of major languages in their **descending** order of usage:

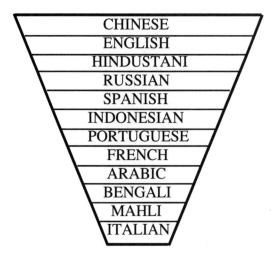

CHINESE
ENGLISH
HINDUSTANI
RUSSIAN
SPANISH
INDONESIAN
PORTUGUESE
FRENCH
ARABIC
BENGALI
MAHLI
ITALIAN

Unless implications are carefully analyzed, these languages can very quickly translate a name into sensitive signals; messages of love; hate; insults and profanity; ethnic slurs, and other terribly dangerous connotations.

And yet. . .

## COINED NAMES HAVE TAKEN OFF!

The reasons for the explosive increase in coined names are numerous and critical: American businesses have expanded at an unpredicted rate, making good, new names increasingly difficult to register. In addition, after companies would attain dominant market share domestically, they sought international markets as a source of growth.

These factors forced creative marketers to develop new corporate identities which were more generic and combined interesting sounds with unique "alpha" structures--such as the now widely accepted KODAK and XEROX.

The downside, for a change, was **not** a limiting or stultifying quality to these names, but merely the fact that it was increasingly difficult for companies to find three-or-four-letter combinations which had not already been registered, or were pronounceable, or were not easily mistaken for **other** alpha-combinations which were already in use.

Coined names obviously require strong linguistic and overall naming expertise; otherwise, poor alpha-combinations could do great harm to a corporation's image.

## SILLY NAMES

In Dallas, Texas, a chain of 57 stores across the south and west of the U.S. closes seven months a year, because they find that most consumers do not purchase gifts and linen year-round. The store is called **TUESDAY MORNING**, and opens seven days a week (five months a year). They have that name because its founder and chairman believes that Tuesday is the "most positive" day of the week. Maybe so. But at least one dozen times every day, each one of the 57 stores receives a call which asks: "Are you open today?" **(7-11 is open 24 hours a day.)**

# CASE STUDY:

## A BRAND NEW NAME FOR
## AN OLD INSTITUTION

Recently, we received a call from the naming committee of a respected, nearly one-century-old financial institution.  It was a $50-billion company, which had recently sold large chunks of its assets to a $60-billion bank.

The committee consisted of a corporate representative, a legal representative, and a public affairs representative, all gathered for the express purpose of replacing their name, which **had** to be changed, due to its recent actions.

In every sense, this was a giant company, with over 200 ventures around the globe, and even a small bank in England.  My mandate was clear: to find a name which categorically had **nothing** to do with its previous incarnation:  I could not use ROYAL, TRUST, CANADA, BLUE or BANK, since the firm was determined to break out of its geographic limitations, and needed a strong disassociation with its past.

At the same time, the institution wanted a name which would be world-class, elite, powerful, and transparent--the latter meaning that it had no dictionary meaning.  The name had to, as well, be highly suitable for international financial services, and be continued to be seen and used by both banks and trust companies.

In order to achieve that flexibility in a great rush and panic, I quickly got the team going. We had three meetings in less than two weeks, and were able to place a short list of names before the board. These names were all globally protectable, and had been acceptable to everyone on the naming committee.

Thus was **GENTRA** created, with all of its implications of gentry, gentrification, gentlemen, gentle, yet also strength and tradition. And today, the name GENTRA handles a multi-billion dollar portfolio around the world.

## A NAME THAT DIDN'T FLY

A totally idiotic way of accomplishing a name change is to do what a once-important airline company did:

In the spring of 1987, United Airlines chose a leading identity firm, which created a name using focus groups: "Allegis."

So what happened?

$7 million was spent on Allegis advertising.

Donald Trump, of real estate fame, declared that the new name "Sounds like the next world-class disease." (And he owned 5% of the company stock, too.)

A month and a half later, the Allegis board dumped its chairman, Richard J. Ferris, and replaced him with Frank A. Olson.

In one of his first acts, Olson announced that he planned to dump the new name Allegis, and change the company's name **back** to United Airlines Inc.

The new name had lasted just over six weeks, which is a shorter life span than several kinds of fruitflies whose Latin names are even **harder** to pronounce.

So, it is fascinating to note how more and more companies have turned to coined names over the past few decades. And the use of coined names continues apace, with more and more companies turning to "manufactured" names to try and guarantee that their subsidiaries, products and services carry a personality which is similar to the parent organization.

## COINED

1955                                            1992

34                                              139

Coined names are increasing in use. Only if they are corrected developed, can we list these positive aspects of coined names:

They are unlimited in scope.

They are unlimited in language.

They are completely distinct.

They are completely proprietary.

127

*With the coming of the globalization of commerce, coined names are becoming increasingly desired.*
*But they can be dangerous, if they fail to achieve worldwide language and trademark clearance.*

# Naming Spectrum

**8**

There is a colorful rainbow of other kinds of names. While our lives are filled with millions of products, each business wants to radiate the right color.

*aming, from classical to foreign, from serious to playful, from techie to tacky, from dumb to silly, has been practiced aggressively since the Industrial Revolution.*

*Today, many of these names can only be seen as desperate moments in the history of each company, when they chose, often unwisely, a name which they are forced to live with forever.*

One kind is the **classical**, in which Greek, Roman and even non-Western myths and legends have been drawn upon, to trigger (possible) sub-conscious connections in the minds of customers, or simply to give a millennia-admired name to a new product. And what product does not wish to achieve instant recognition and respect through such associations?

The use of ancient myths and gods has, then, a sort of double-barreled advantage: To use an exotic and impressive-sounding name for those who are **not** aware of the story behind it, and to give an extra level of meaning for those who **are**. So, while tens of millions can still sing the TV jingle of the 1950s about the household cleaner Ajax ("boom-boom--the foaming cleanser! Boom-boom-boom," etc.), probably only a fraction of that number are aware that Ajax was a Greek soldier who fought boldly and bravely in the Trojan War.

The examples are almost as numerous as ancient myths themselves--except perhaps Hades, for who wants a company or product which refers to Hell and the Underworld? Long before Mercury became a proud member of the Ford family of automobiles--even long before it became the name of a planet in our solar system--it was a speedy messenger god.

(Providing a wonderful excuse to the traffic cop who pulls you over on the highway: "I couldn't help it, officer; it's a Mercury.")

Vulcan, well known as the Roman blacksmith god, made a superior choice as the name for metal products, as well as a kind of processed rubber.

## JAPANESE NAMES

Brand names in Japan include:

**POCKET WETTY**
pre-moistened hand towelettes

**COW BRAND**
Shampoo

**CALPIS**
soft drink

**MORE RAN**
tea cakes

**NAIL REMOVER**
fingernail cleaner

**TRIM PECKER**
trousers

**POCARI SWEAT**
soft drink

**SHOT VISION**
TV sets

131

## IS ENGLISH TAKING OVER THE WORLD?

The impact of the English language as the new "lingua franca" cannot be over-estimated:

In France, the French insist on calling the computer "ordinateur," but in Italy, everyone calls it by its American name.

French magazines now use terms such as "le trekking" and "le rafting."

Italians love to talk about "il body building."

And Germans, naturally, love to go out for "das Joggen."

Ditto for a whirlpool bath called Adonis, named for a beautiful young Greek lad of antiquity; there is a brand name for tripods (and probably a thousand other products) called Hercules, after the mythical Greek hero who was well known for his magnificent strength, and so on.

Interestingly, many other cultures have been successfully drawn upon for their gods and goddesses' names. For instance, Mazda is the persona of the Persian god of light, which made it an inspired tag for a brand of light bulb many years ago, but is now far more familiar as a widely-selling Japanese-made automobile.

The problem with business names drawn from what I call classical sources is soon clear: There are a limited number of them; they would be difficult to avoid being considered either generic or proprietary; nearly all "good" ones have long ago been taken.

The advantage of business names taken from **foreign languages** is much like that of coined words like "KODAK": they are not immediately, if ever, understood by consumers.

Indeed, words from other languages can often create a kind of "sophisticated" impression, in the same way that many of us are charmed and even thrilled to encounter other people with a flare for speaking and understanding other languages than our own.

The romance languages, particularly French and Italian, have often provided a rich trove of "foreign words"--foreign to English-speakers, at least!--and have given us such frequently-used product and business names as Chauffeur, Riunite, Capezio, and Fleur de Lys.

Exotic feelings and images can be conjured up by such names as Kon Tiki, Hai Karate, and Liebfraumilch. And names such as Bambino and Cafe have been easily accepted by the English-speaking consumer.

The mother of countless modern languages, Latin, has **also** proved to be a trustworthy source of good business names. The Latin word for tree, for instance--arbor--yielded the excellent brand name Arborite, for a product which is a kind of imitation of wood.

A far more ancient example, and one with richer echoes for even the **non**-Latin-knowing public, would be Aquascutum, which has been "around" since 1853. The term comes from the Latin word and means "Water-Shield," which seems like a perfectly logical choice for a line of rainwear. It may have pronunciation problems, but it's unique and distinct quality has proven it to be a superb product name. (Furthermore, what English-speaker does not have images of "aquarium," "aqua-lung" and "aquatic" come to mind, when hearing the term Aquascutum, even if he/she is utterly unaware of the original Latin word for "water" is aqua?)

## NAMES OF MOVIES

During the 1980s, two major art films, with music composed by Philip Glass, were released around the world. They were called: **KOYAANISQATSI** and **POWAQQATSI.** Both received excellent reviews; neither made much money. After all, how could one even call the box office and ask what time uh, er, um, well, "Whatsit" started?? Never mind asking a video store if they have a copy for rent, or if they have even **heard** of it.

Clearly, these are two examples of what we mean when we say "names beyond recognition."

Other examples of using Latin abound, such as Nivea, from the original word "niveus," meaning snowy. What better name for a white, cool skin cream?

Foreign languages, then, such as Latin and its many derivatives, have provided--and probably will continue to provide--many names for products and even companies.

Another trend in business naming is what I call the **alpha-numeric** kind. This sounds far more sophisticated then it is; it simply means **using letters and numbers to form a name for a company, service or product.**

The most famous example would be the corporate name change--telescoping, really-- of the major international conglomerate Minnesota Mining and Manufacturing Company to 3M. (which gives one a powerful example of the limitations of a geographic name, doesn't it? How would Japan or Germany relate to a strange, native Indian name such as "Minnesota"?)

3M has, of course, become almost as generic as Scotch-Tape and Klennex tissue, and is living proof that an alpha-numeric moniker is often far better than an acronym, or a coined word based on its old name, such as "MinMin."

Numbers in combination with letters or words have often been used, and quite successfully, to name products.

Examples abound: A-1 STEAK SAUCE
calls forth images of quality and "the best";
2ND DEBUT implies youth and another
chance; 7-UP suggests lifting a bottle or glass
to one's lips; 9 LIVES CAT FOOD plays on the
almost-universal image of kittens and cats having
many lives, from dodging cars to falling from
great heights and always landing on their feet.

Other alpha-numerics lack such conscious or sub-
conscious meaning, but have still "caught on"
with the general public, regardless of this
hook-less-ness. RUB A-535 is one example;
the "A" might carry echoes of what our parents
urged us to earn in school--but why the 535?

There have actually been several successful
consumer items which go by the "name" of
numbers, alone. Germany produces a cologne
called **4711**; and there is an **1878 Rye**. The
latter, at least, might give a sub-conscious
implication that the firm has been churning
the drink out for over a century.

Still, the problems of alpha-numerics are as
numerous as the possibilities of letter/number
combinations. For one thing, imagine the
confusion in the marketplace if all--or even
many--products were simply numbered!

There are legal ramifications as well. How
can a company prevent the use of a number
by another firm? Obviously, it cannot.

## A SILLY NAME

There is a new hair
product company
from France, with
a global product line
called

**PHYTOTHERATHRIE.**

You will be relieved
to know that it has
been legally
protected, and
is a registered
trademark.

Furthermore, a number provides absolutely **zero** identification with goods or services in the mind of the public; quite the contrary, a numbered-product is more likely to cultivate feelings of mystery, mistrust, and even communist-type images of de-personalization.

The frequent images of university students complaining that "I'm only a number in this place!" captures the danger inherent in this. As does the classic Hollywood line of the criminal in Alcatraz declaring "Prisoner Number 3 requests permission to cross the white line, sir."

There is a further troublesome aspect to alpha-numeric names. Human memory can only handle so many numbers in a row, and a long string of them can easily alienate the public. **Words** have meanings, of course, and even nonsense words such as EXXON are capable of taking on meaning, if only by association and through repetition. Numbers, however, lack the quality--something to be remembered by anyone who wishes to name their company or product in this fashion.

A further kind of business naming is what I like to call **Variations.** This is an extremely simple naming device, based on the most obvious kind of thinking: To alter the spelling of something ever-so-slightly, whether by omitting a syllable to make it "breezier," or by changing a letter or two, to make it more memorable.

The two most frequent examples of this--and which you probably saw several dozen examples of, driving your car of taking the bus to work this morning--would be spelling "new" as "NU," or turning "quality" into "KWALITEE."

Such strangely spelled words can be strung together, of course, to have widely ranging effects upon the consumer. These deviant spellings can be eye-catching (even if they drive language purists haff-kray-zee), and have often been used to help distinguish similarly-named products in the ever-expanding marketplace.

Some of these variations, or deviations of spelling, have been based on regional pronunciations. For example, in New York City and other accent-filled locations in the eastern United States, names such as Neva-Lose, Wonda-Cloth and Kleer-Wite may be found.

Other variations in pronunciation (and spelling) have produced such product names as Bit O' Honey, Faskota, Thun Thoot, and Gli-Door.

Another common method used to create business names of this genre consists of the substitution of letters, or numbers, for words. We see this most clearly in names such as **X**-pert, **E**-**Z**FLO, CANT-**B**-LOST, **U**-**C**-lite, and fitz-**M**-ALL. The most famous one of all is now utterly generic and a long-accepted word in any modern dictionary: BAR-**B**-**Q**.

## LUCKY HONG KONG NAMES

Some names of companies found in the Hong Kong phone book:

**EverRich Inc.**

**Great Profit Co.**

**Great Success Inc.**

**EverydayLucky Co.**

How can they possibly **fail**??

And let us not forget the ever-popular tradition
in names to replace the word "to" with the
number 2, and to shorten the word "for"
into the number 4.

Other product and service names rely on a
simplified spelling, which choose to eliminate
supposedly "unnecessary" letters, in order to get
across the idea in a faster, more unique fashion.
The examples of these could fill the rest of the
pages of this book: SNO SHOO.  DUAEZY.
TUF-GRIP.  GOURMAY.  STA-TRU.
D'ZERT.  DED-N-DUN.

Then there are the consumer products given
names which are made to look "different"--
even at the risk of ten thousand English teachers
longing to strangle the creators of these words--
through substituting vowel graphemes :
EVURREADY.  HYGEEN.  NEET.

Other names of products have been created
through similar manipulation of consonants:
MAJIC.  KLEAN.  FOLDZTITE.
RUFF & TUFF.  Ad infinitum!

Names can also use literary devices such as witty
puns, to grab the attention of the consumer:
SEIZER as the brand name of a clamp, for
instance, plays on the word "CAESAR,"
as well as "SEIZE HER."

Then there are often hilarious names for stores, such as:

● CLOTHES ENCOUNTERS

● THE SAUCERER'S APPRENTICE

● SIR PLUS

And almost everyone's favorite:
THE BRICK SHIRT HOUSE. All of these cleverly play on familiar words and common expressions, movie titles, and so on.

Other kinds of name variations have less humorous origins, but have often proven to be masterful choices: Standard Oil being shortened to S.O., and then molded into ESSO, is one renowned example. As we noted in our automobile-naming chapter, the dully-named "general-purpose vehicle" from World War II quickly was shortened to G. P., which soon became JEEP. And how many on this earth are aware that the endless chemical name of Poly-**te**tra-**fl**uor**o**-ethyl**e**ne yielded the name TEFLON, by placing together its 5th, 6th, 10th, 11th, 15th and 22nd letters? Talk about inspired variations!

## ANIMATION OF NAMES

In 1988, NBC brought back its peacock, after years of using a stylized "N."

Ditto Exxon's tiger.

Ditto Hartford Insurance's stag.

Of course, RCA's little listening dog never left.

Sometimes, in creating variations, we encounter a combination of different kinds of naming. For instance, the long-popular BRYLCREEM come from a hair dressing preparation, "brilliantine," along with a stylized variant spelling of the word "cream."

Whether the name is created through an extensive process of rearrangement; whether it was born by twisting sounds, adding letters, dropping syllables, or through the miniaturization of lengthy concepts using acronyms and prefixes, one thing is certain:

**The Art lies not in inventing these names, but in matching ideas with a few letters of a symbol, which can then convey an image to the potential consumer in an appropriate and memorable manner.**

# NAMING HANG-OVERS

Names become all the more crucial in the world of wines. There might be up to 200 different Chardonnays made in California, and consumers can hardly be expected to taste every one of them. So, many of them have learned to trade on family names and strong personalities, to make their wines stand out on the shelves.

The proprietary nature of wine names is often in the courts. In the fall of 1993, a Paris court ruled that Yves Saint Laurent had **no** right to use the name "Champagne" for a new perfume. The company had actually spent $17-million on advertising for the fragrance, before losing the right to use the name in France. In the meantime, court decisions are pending in other countries, pushing all marketing into a costly limbo.

Internationally, many wine "names" have become generic. In 1933, Canada and France concluded a trade agreement to protect such French appellations of origin as Bordeaux, Burgundy, and Champagne. But in 1980, that treaty was cancelled by the Canadian Parliament, eliminating protection in that country for names-of-origin wines.

Still, there are always the possibilities for infringement. Inniskillin Wines Inc. of Canada found that Beaujolais Nouveau was becoming confused with their own Vin Nouveau. A name change was made in 1979 without a single law suit or lawyer becoming necessary.

## VODKA NAME

A European vodka named **Black Death** was briefly imported into the U.S. by a California distributing company until 1989, when the U.S. Treasury decided to ban it from the country. The action was apparently taken because the name, and its logo (a grinning skull), created a "misleading impression of bubonic plaque and poison." One man's meat, etc.

## NAMING GAMES

When one looks at the names of the over 100 teams in pro basketball, baseball, hockey and football, a number of trends starts to emerge.

MACHO NAMES:  Some one-fourth of sport names radiate this quality, from hockey's New York Rangers to football's Minnesota Vikings to baseball's Pittsburgh Pirates --all of them implying that pro team sports are not only played by men, but appeal primarily to that sex, as well. A more historical macho name is that taken by the Canadian Football League's Toronto Argonauts, based on the ancient Greek legend of the guys who set off their own, prize-winning odyssey.

GEOGRAPHICAL / HISTORICAL / INDUSTRIAL NAMES:  Examples abound in this second-most-popular name category for pro-teams, including the Milwaukee Brewers, the Edmonton Oilers, the Phoenix Suns and the Philadelphia 76ers--all brilliantly drawing upon both geography, history, and even local industries.  This has its risks, of course, just as 3M once longed to be disassociated from Minnesota-alone imagery: Los Angeles lacks lakes, yet it has the Los Angeles Lakers, a successful team with that name.

Long-time fans will remember that the team **first** began in Minneapolis, "the land of 1,000 lakes," so when it moved to L.A., the now-irrelevant name "stuck."

### LADY DI

Lady Di
Dry Cleaners is a small chain of four shops in southern California.
When the British Consulate-General in Los Angeles complained, the owners refused
to drop their name, **or** the line which claims "cleaners to the Royal Family," and told all those who were offended to ask for "a little less starch in their laundry."

This happened again, when the thoughtfully-
named basketball team New Orleans Jazz was
moved to Utah in 1979, where it was decided to
keep the now-unrelated name for continuity-sake.

ANIMAL NAMES: Predators make number 3
on the pro-teams hit list, not surprisingly,
ranging from the Detroit Tigers to the
Minnesota Timberwolves. True, There are no
Rochester Rodents or Chattanooga Chickens--
but there is a beloved team called the
Pittsburgh Penguins, a hard-edged steel town
named after a flightless, awkward bird.
(You guessed: It was chosen by a public contest
held back in 1967, when the team joined the
National Hockey League. At least the
"Pittsburgh Pigs" failed to win, thank heavens.)

Names can change in meaning over the years,
of course, which can lead to **some** potential
heartache. The now-embarrassing ethnic names
of the Atlanta Braves and the Cleveland Indians
are still proudly worn by and cheered on by
millions; and how about the Washington Bullets
of the NBA, which originally got its name from
the munitions factory in Baltimore which once
backed the team?

Today, real bullets fly over drug deals on the
streets of America's Murder Capital/National
Capital--yet the name Washington Bullets
remains one to, uh, kill for.

**KFC**

In Iran, most speak
the Farsi tongue,
which is why
many were upset
to see the
**Finger-licking
good** slogan of a
the fast food giant.

They read it as
**it's so good
you will eat
your fingers**.

## NAMING GENDERS

For businesses, products and services are something which have grown in importance over the past few years, as both feminism, and the inevitable flow of women into the North American (and world) work force, have made necessary.

## POWER OF LETTERS

Recent research, along with centuries of name-study, have suggested that the first letters of companies--and products--carry certain connotations for certain people:

**A**--Achiever
**B**--Compromiser
**C**--Consistent
**D**--Fanciful
**E**--Optimistic
**F**--Active
**G**--Restless

Continued on next page

To put it bluntly: As our consciousness has been raised (to use the feminist phrase), so have the number of problems which many consumers have with certain names similarly increased. We are not merely talking about "political correctness" here; we are talking about nothing less than the alienation of some 54% of the human race, and what is often 75% and more of the purchasing public: the female sex.

More and more companies have begun to aggressively drop product names which seem to have a gender bias.

Furthermore, when business are about to choose a new name, they are considering the female consumer to a greater extent than ever before. After all, women are the largest consumers, and a formidable force in what goes into our refrigerators, closets, and stomachs.

Not only are many store and product names possibly offensive, they often lack any sense of originality and proprietary nature. Some interesting numbers for your non-sexist, gender-sensitive information: There are **over 100** companies and services in North America with the name of "Mr. Clean."

And that does not even include the most famous one of all, which makes your floors so shiny and new-looking.

And keeping with the "Mr." usage: In North America there are some 5,730 which begin with that respectful abbreviation, ranging from Mr. Submarine to Mr. Transmission to Mr. Muffler to thousands of others.

Nor is "Mr." the only possible male-oriented image in a name. How about "king?" Hold you breath here: There are fully 53,573 U.S. businesses or products with the word "king" in their name, of whom the most famous is probably BURGER KING. Nor is the male sex limited to these two images, as can be seen in the world famous LA-Z-BOY, and the major hardware/home improvement chain, Canadian Tire, which chose the male-oriented "MOTOMASTER" as its brand name.

**H**--Determined
**I**--Egotistical
**J**--Fair
**K**--Acquisitive
**L**--Indecisive
**M**--Artistic
**N**--Fatalistic
**O**--Reactive
**P**--Conformist
**Q**--Inquisitive
**R**--Rudimentary
**S**--Status quo
**T**--Uncommitted
**U**--Protective
**V**--Charismatic
**W**--Traditionalist
**X**--Reserved
**Y**--Anonymous
**Z**--Noticeable

Please feel free to invent your **own** interpretations!

## GENDER SENSITIVITY

After a full century as the AMERICAN WAREHOUSEMEN'S ASSOCIATION, the group changed its name (in 1992) to the AMERICAN WAREHOUSE ASSOCIATION. Noted its president, "The number of women owners, managers and employees in the industry has increased dramatically over the years. Therefore, we felt the change was necessary."

You've come a long way, boys.

Indeed, in the city of Toronto, Canada alone-- which has fewer than 4 million souls in its greater metropolitan area--there are over 200 companies listed in its phone book which begin with Mr., ranging from MISTER AIR DUCT to MR. ZAK'S CONVENIENCE.

Are these names **necessarily** offensive to over one-half of our population, in the way that, say, the image of the beaming, toothy, black Aunt Jemima on a pancake box has become for many Afro-Americans? Will Mr. Clean have to clean up his act?

(After all, for better or for worse, 95% of those who purchase and use Mr. Clean are undoubtedly women!) And when an American is in the mood for a cookie, need he/she prefer David's over Mrs. Fields, because the latter possesses a prefix which has echoes of pre-feminist, pre-"Ms." times?

Not necessarily. One has trouble imagining even the most passionate feminist driving an extra mile to McDonald's, in order to avoid eating at a place with a (possibly) sexiest name like "Burger King." Yet one can imagine a company name such as "Molly Maid" (a fast growing firm which provides domestic cleaning service for the growing number of homes where both husband and wife work outside the house) being considered old-fashioned and even off-putting.

One thing is abundantly clear:  The changing role of women in most Western societies has added one more concern to the appropriateness of names for both businesses and products, as well as services.  Which leads us to a further trend--in both society in general, and naming in particular.

## DIFFERENT MEANINGS OF GESTURES

When one signals with thumb and forefinger in the U.S., the sweet circle means "O.K."

In Japan, it means "money."

But in France, it means "worthless."

And in Brazil, it's downright obscene.

So much for the ads for that chain of hotels, in which a guest gives the sign to the concierge, with his happy/wealthy/ cheap/filthy fingers.

147

## NAMING ECOLOGY

**Environmental concerns** have led to the
veritable explosion of business and product
names which risk dreadful over-use of datedness.

Please do not get me wrong here: The growing,
world-wide concern, even obsession, with saving
the ozone layer and preserving our rapidly
depleting environment, is both laudable and
admirable.

The question is, how far should business go in
choosing names which reflect this concern?
And at what point has the perfectly legitimate
desire to acknowledge this trend led to soon-to-
be-forgotten-and-overused-names?

Certainly, one can keep up with science, nature
and the environment by reading the fine
**Discovery Magazine**, which is well named and
suggests its contents adequately. But then if you
charge the cost of that periodical on your
DISCOVER CREDIT CARD,
what does this say to us?

One can use TREEFREE tissues, which reflects
the environmental concerns of many of us.
And you can use that product to wipe away
UNPETROLEUM jelly cream, which might
make one feel good about not using a non-
renewable resource.

Still, look at the dreadful repetition and lack of uniqueness which has now flooded the marketplace, in a sincere effort to respect and reflect this growing global sensitivity!

To prove your profound interest in ecology, one can become involved in either ENVIROCAR or ENVIRONQUEST projects. One can drop one's subscription to the **Wall Street Journal** and take out ones for:

- MOTHER JONES
- E MAGAZINE
- NEW ENVIRONMENT

You can stroll through your neighborhood park with an ECOSAC in which to place all of your litter, and then when you've returned home, rake your leaves into an ECOBAG.

Your conscience can remain clear, if you choose to purchase and use ECOCHOICE or ECOBELLA body care products in your bedroom and washroom. And, when at the supermarket, there are always GREEN products to buy--since there were, as of the end of 1990-- over 1,350 with that name, along with dozens of ecologically-related political parties around the world.

## HAPPY CAN

In Hong Kong, the Cantonese word for Coke is **Hou Hau Hou Lok.** The Chinese characters mean "Delicious Fun," as well as "Tastes good for your mouth," and even "Delicious Happy Can."

## ROCKY NAMES

A group by any other name would just be noise. Speaking about rock bands, a major critic once noted: "Groups pick the kind of names your parents would hate."

See if you agree:

- THE LAUGHING KHADAFYS
- ATTILA THE STOCKBROKER
- MENTAL FLOSS
- DEAD BRAIN CELLS
- USELESS AND FRUSTRATED
- JELLYFISH BABIES
- VERBAL ASSAULT
- MEN THEY COULDN'T HANG
- HALF MAN / HALF BISCUIT
- PIG FARM

And for all of you capitalists out there :

- DOW JONES AND THE INDUSTRIALISTS

Louise Chiccone strategically found the holiest name for herself: MADONNA.

And another world-famous group took the expression "in excess," and turned it into the catchy initials INXS.

## PEPPER KID

Tabasco's Hong Kong advertising agency, which will remain nameless, chose the name **Sin Mai Goh** for this product-- which means "fresh, tasty paste."

True, it was catchy and phonetic, but Tabasco is **not** a paste, and consumers rebelled.

Its eventual name became **Lat Djiew Jai**, which means **Pepper Kid**.

## NAMING GOLD

Which leads me to a not-unrelated phenomenon
of dreadful over-use: the word "GOLD."

When a name trend turns into a cliché, it is time
for businesses and corporations to take heed.
One such example was the veritable **gold-rush**
of the 1980s, which was even more frenetic than
the ECO/ENVIRO/GREEN movement which is
still on.

So, you could get GOLDSEAL SERVICE at
such places as the GOLDEN NUGGET CASINO
during the last decade. And, understandably, you
could pay for it with your American Express
Gold Card. Or your Gold Master Card.
Or your Gold Visa Card, for that matter.

You could then go out to your car and start it up
with your GOLDKEY, and, when necessary, fill
'er up with SHELL GOLD or SUNOCO GOLD
gasoline. You could also enjoy those special
perks which come from flying place to place
as a GOLDCLUB MEMBER, secure in the
knowledge that your GOLDDOME bank account
would always cover the tab.

I needn't use the golden opportunity to go on.
As we moved into the 90s, all those ubiquitous
Gold names began to lose their glitter, and started
to leave a rather metallic taste in the mouths of
many millions of consumers.

### 7-UP

7-Up is called
**Chat Hai** in
Cantonese.
True, Chat means
"seven," and
Hai can mean
"bubbles,"
"happiness," and
even "yes."

However, if
it's spoken with
a certain musical
tone, it means
something very
nasty and rude.
What a world!

151

By the end of the last decade, there were more than 3,800 trademarks registered in the U.S. for consumer products and services with the name "GOLD" as a prefix. (Of course, the **truly** successful members of society's elite had already begun to embrace PLATINUM credit and services, in a futile attempt to distinguish themselves from everyone else.)

Is there no SILVER lining to the clouds all around product/service/business naming? Probably not.

Of course, when all of these over-used and over-heard names are long forgotten, businesses can fall back to earth, where that big GREEN, ECOLOGICALLY-SAFE cushion awaits them.

## NAMING FUNCTIONS

This may be a worthwhile place to study how names of products or companies can reflect their function.

Names which show what products can do:

- AQUA VELVA

- BUG OFF

- CLOSE-UP TOOTHPASTE

Names which suggest how little work we humans have to do:

- EASY ON

- EASY OFF

- LESTOIL

- ONE WIPE

Names which reflect how little time we have, and how fast products work:

- QUICK FLOW

- QUICK START

- JETSET

Names which reflect class distinction:

- KNIGHT
- CASTLE
- PRINCE MATCHABELLI
- CREST
- CORDON BLEU

Name which reflect bargains:

- THRIFTY
- ECONOPAC

Names which imply precision, or long-lasting qualities:

- ACCUMATIC
- ACCUPRINT
- DURASHINE
- DURACELL

*In conclusion, as you can see, there are countless varieties of names for companies and products. The question and goal remains: How to choose the correct name for the marketing strategy?*

# The Highs and Lows of Hi-Tech Naming

9

Whether we take a
bite of APPLE or
open or close the
WINDOWS, there
are real problems
with computer
naming.

*he billion dollar hangover of Microsoft is one of the most extraordinary examples of how a great company can harm itself terribly through casual naming.*

Imagine if Dupont ran full-page ads, warning businesses not to use the word "nylon" in any association with their products. Or General Foods started to warn the world not to use the word "Jello" to describe their desserts. Well, here comes Microsoft, the greatest success story of the 20th Century, filling international media with an advertisement in the fall of 1993 which read as follows:

---

**WINDOWS.**

**IT'S OVER 2 MILLION LINES OF CODE.**

**IT'S INSTALLED ON OVER 30 MILLION PCs.**

**IT'S MICROSOFT'S TRADEMARK.**

---

Here they are, **begging** their competitors to "be gentle" with the use of the word WINDOWS in association with other products. The book you are reading has been produced using this superb Microsoft WINDOWS product. It's a remarkable hi-tech system.

Yet sometimes, even the most famous names can be successfully challenged for their propriety, as can be seen in this case. Understandably, Microsoft wanted to trademark the word WINDOWS, but the U.S. Patent and Trademark Office rejected the request. In a letter to the billion-dollar software company, they declared that the word "windows" had a special meaning for computer users for many years **before** Microsoft released its first version of the product, ten years earlier. "The evidence clearly demonstrates that the public understands the term windows to mean a genus of goods, namely computer software which utilizes windows on a computer screen," it argued.

(In this, it echoed the rationale of earlier rulings, which refused to allow trademarks of such other widely-accepted terms as "the Pill" and "Light," "Dry," and "Ice" beer.)

As of the spring of 1993, Microsoft was appealing the decision, claiming that the word "windows" is now strongly linked to their product--and with good reason: If the company **did** have legal control over the word "windows," it could require any future manufacturers to be licensed by Microsoft before releasing Windows-compatible software.

It's the sort of thing which periodically reoccurs every few years in the world of business: We've seen it with "Formica," "Thermos," and "Fridge."

A case in point is what happened to "Xerox."

Back in the 1950s, when xeroxography was discovered, it was given the name "Xerox," a moniker based purely on its technological origin. Undoubtedly, the name was extremely odd and difficult, but the company's commitment to utilize its uniqueness as a mark of global identity led them to establish a textbook pro-active corporate identity program.

Unlike Microsoft, which not only picked up a dictionary word, but failed to establish a world-wide proprietary system around it, Xerox never allowed any company which produced a bond paper copier to even come **close** to its principal technology; i.e. xeroxography, to be used--such as:

- ZEROGRAPHY
- PROZEROX
- XEROXSYS

You can see the result in the photocopy industry of today:

- APECO
- CANON
- MINOLTA
- SHARP

--but nothing anywhere near to the term "xeroxography."

And then there was the propriety dilemma of the genii over at Intel. True, "286" was a rather technical number to end up as the product name of a cutting edge microchip in the mid-80s, and they decided to **not** name their subsequent products 287, 288 and so on, but rather they jumped by hundreds, like car makers do:

- **386**

- **486**

- **586**, etc.

In the interim, understandably, companies all over the globe quickly registered **all sorts** of numbers--such as 386, 486, 586, 686, 786, 886, 986, and so on, often correctly anticipating the subsequent models which would be produced by Intel.

## "I.Q." IS A CONFUSING NAME

Bell Atlantic has a new business system called Intelligentnetwor**Q**, with the "**I**" and the "**Q**" capitalized.

But do many of us have the **IQ** to figure that out??

Thus, the creative hi-tech manufacturer could **not** bring out, successfully, 586, 686, 786, and so on, since they were not clearly available world-wide.

And here now comes PENTIUM as a purported solution, and a substitute for 586. But Intel had better be careful, once again:

- SEXTIUM
- SEPTIUM
- OCTIUM

have undoubtedly been registered internationally, just waiting to pounce.

And the saga continues!

In the 1990s, the hi-tech names which will be filling our newspapers will be such monikers as:

- IRIDIUM
- POWERFONE
- CABELTEL
- PICTURETEL
- UNITEL

and countless others. One hopes that these names will survive the endless dilution, confusion and lack of proprietary protection of the Microsofts and Intels which preceded them to market.

# CASE STUDY:

## RE-ENGINEERING OF AN ENGINEERING SUCCESS

In 1993, we were called by IBM Canada -- the second largest IBM operation in the world outside the United States, with some 12,000 employees. This subsidiary is recognized as a leader in the field, with its own independent innovations, technologies, and standards.

As part of its restructuring, the manufacturing facilities of IBM Canada were about to become an independent spin-off and global player in micro-electronics. And it needed a new name.

The company went through the normal routine -- internal naming, contests, focus groups -- you name it!

Then, we were called in. By the time I arrived, there were 1200 names already rejected by the naming committee for being too long, too short, too narrow, too difficult, etc. Good ones were available in America, but not worldwide. A lot of time and energy had gone into this intense exercise.

When we were briefed on this major challenge, the concern was clear: to find a name which was futuristic, stylish, and positively registerable worldwide.

Within two weeks, we developed the name **CELESTICA** as a final candidate. We were able to quickly obtain full support from the CEO, IBM legal department, public relations, advertising, and their corporate identity team, all of whom cheered for its success.

At the end of 1993, this name was released world-wide, with international press conferences. The Toronto-based manufacturing company was spun off, with a new name; it was still wholly owned by IBM, but would someday become privatized.

So, out of the blue, into the top ranks of contract manufacturing, CELESTICA, a billion-dollar enterprise with over seventy-five years experience manufacturing for IBM, was launched with a logo depicted as a fireball.

## WHERE WERE ALL THESE NAMING PROBLEMS COMING FROM? THE DAWN OF HI-TECH NAMING

Several years ago, **The New Yorker** magazine had a quite extraordinary cartoon. It consisted of a photograph of a little old lady, surrounded by some two dozen young children, sitting in front of a schoolhouse.

The large caption beneath read (something like):

### MISS MATILDA JOHNSON'S SECOND GRADE CLASS.

And beneath that, the names of the children in the "photo" were listed: Jennifer, Jeremy, Jennifer, Jennifer, Jennifer, Miss Johnson, Jennifer, Jeremy, Jennifer. And in the second row: Jeremy, Jennifer, Jennifer, Jeremy, Jennifer, Jennifer, Jennifer, Jeremy, Jennifer.

The "gag" is quickly and uproariously made: There is a tendency for human societies to latch onto certain names over periods of time, and stick them to our beloved offspring. Nor is this limited to "given" names, of course; turn to the name "Jones" in any phone book in Wales; "Wong" in China; "Singh" in Sikh communities in India. You will find this also shown to be true.

And then, there are the names for computer companies and products!

When it was High Noon for the hi-tech industry, ABC Namebank undertook a major study to monitor the naming influences of the period. In an analysis of over 175,000 American companies which were then manufacturing nearly one-million (!) computer hardware and software products, it was discovered that most companies were using a strikingly similar group of names.

The following were some of the over-used terms in the computer industry:

**Sys** appeared in **173,300** names.
**Comm** was used within **50,670** names.
**Info** could be found in **26,400** names.
**Data** made it into **26,070** names.
**Soft** was within **17,530** names.
**Tech** appeared in **17,013** names.
**Micro**, within **11,027** names.
**Link**, in **2,770** names.
**Net**, within **1,540** names.

Oh, dear, oh dear, oh dear. Consumers in the '80s and '90s must feel an awful lot like dear old Matilda Johnson, when she tries to call on a boy or girl in her Grade 2 class.

The problem is as evident as the nose on your face and the mouse on your desk:

**The rapid rise of the computer industry led to a sloppiness and repetitiveness in naming-- which, in turn, led to diluted and confused market recognition of companies and their products.**

**To be fair, that rapidity--explosion, really--in the electronic information market has been <u>so</u> astounding, it is amazing that many companies could find the time to slap any monikers on their products at all!  We have gone from an air-conditioned room filled with massive hardware, to a 486 palm-top, almost overnight.**

What my extensive research -- done on poorly-named computer products, of course -- showed me, was that the computer industry has become littered with more acronyms and alpha-numeric jargon then all the secret code words used throughout the Second World War!

There is a catch here, of course:  The purpose of those secret code words in World War II was to confuse, confound, and enrage the enemy.  I have always assumed that the purpose of any company or product name is to enlighten, entice and charm the potential customer.

Indeed, as early as 1983, I was being quoted in the international computer press as saying, "Over 80% of North American computer company names are no good."

Everywhere one looked, a full decade ago, the majority of names were actually **generic**, such as:

- DATACOM
- DATA GENERAL
- DATALINE
- DATATECH
- DATATRON
- DATASYS

and so on.

Furthermore, many were identical in part to each other's names, and had been merely rearranged to create purportedly **new** names!

True, certain words were believed (by everyone!) in the hi-tech industry to be conveying "high quality," "professionalism," and "scientific achievement" to the general public. And, at first glance, they seemed to be superior marketing names. But the industry had grown too quickly to not mean that at least a portion of a company name selected had **already** been chosen, and used, by **another** computer firm to identify its products!

And how about the wonderful, useful services offered by:

- INFOSYS
- INFOFAX
- INFOMART
- INFOTRON
- INFO-TECH
- INFOTEK
- INFOGLOBE
- INFOBYTE
- INFOCOM
- INFOFICHE

Back in the mid-80s, every one of those firms were competing in the North American marketplace. I would hate to try and discover how many are still with us today.

And how many would blame their uninspired choices of company names as a major reason for why they failed to survive?

## WHAT IS YOURS,
## MAY WELL BE MINE!

You see, there is a common misconception on the part of many new or small companies: "Once a name is registered locally, it is legally ours, and unusable anywhere in the North American marketplace."

Of course, not **all** firms change their names when forced to, due to legal struggles. But the computer industry certainly had to solve its naming problems, and at the speed of light, if possible.

## THE UPPER AND LOWER-CASE DISEASE OF TECHIES: nVIEW, dAVID, and mORE

Now, wHAT the hELL does **tHAT** mean, **hUH?**

There is a general misconception in the hi-tech industry, that using a lower-case character in a name creates some kind of a differentiation or distinction in a name.  So, if "DAVID SOFTWARE" is already taken, you can simply become "dAVID SYSTEM."  They are **wrong!** Trademark law does not recognize upper and lower cases, nor does it acknowledge dashes or slashes in names.  David is David, in the end.

With nVIEW, there are NETVIEW and VIEWNET.

One of the fastest growing companies in North America is **T² MEDICAL INC.**

Initials.  Acronyms.  And worse:  Software packages with names which have no apparent connection to the function of the product, putting consumers into a perpetual tizzy.

Talk about "user **un**-friendly!"

## TOO MANY INITIALS, TOO MANY NUMBERS, TOO MUCH CONFUSION EVERYWHERE-- INCLUDING I.B.M.

Once again, let's try to be fair to what is still a very young industry: Many hi-tech companies simply did not perceive, in their early years, any need whatsoever to concentrate on their image. When Henry Ford was one of the only names in town, he could slap an "A" or "T" on his family-named cars, paint them black, price 'em cheap, and sell them off to an eager, anticipating public. But when the competition for market share heated up, old Henry quickly realized that he'd better offer other colors and other styles, or else Chevy would leave him in its dust. (As it did, for the next half-century).

Remember the classic cartoon image of the "light bulb" gleaming above a character's head, symbolizing that he or she just "got" a bright idea? (Edison never sued for infringement of copyright, we are safe to assume).

That's what happened over at International Business Machines, a/k/a IBM. Let me quote from a "light bulb" moment which took place in late 1987, when then-CEO John Akers was reviewing the product menu at a meeting, and scanned a list of vague acronyms and numbers piled one after another after another:

"We have **terrible** names!" exploded Akers. "If **I** can't understand what these products do, how can we expect our customers to understand?" Thus began a major new effort to create brand and corporate consistency at the giant conglomerate, of which my company soon became a major part. (And with nearly 10,000 products and services, back in 1989--amounting to an average of **four product introductions every single day**--confusion was abounding both outside and inside Big Blue).

At the time I came on board, IBM--then America's most profitable company--was taking almost four person-years to develop a single mark. Something had to be done.

To deal with their problem quickly and efficiently, I decided to "franchise" my own methodology to the company, which I had been using successfully for a full decade. First, I introduced a detailed system and procedures which were adapted to IBM's very specific needs.

I then organized a comprehensive library of major reference books on language, trends, foreign issues (never forgetting that Chevy's "Nova" means "won't go" in Spanish), and actual histories of naming.

Information about specific trade marks and corporate data was also organized, on-line. I and my associates then trained selected IBM employees to operate what had become IBM's own Naming Reference Center, or NRC. And today, it handles over 1,200 product-related naming issues each year.

I think you get the idea. It took IBM -- and countless other, far less successful computer companies--quite a while to break the unfortunate habit of using generic names and careless treatments of brand names, as a kind of "convenient shorthand." After all, the purpose of shorthand was to speed things up for a secretary; not to confuse bosses, workers and consumers alike.

As one IBM manager declared, "Assigning acronym-based or generic names late in the product cycle, when there was no time to do anything else, became a common practice and an easy way out." Since the late '80s, Big Blue's naming team has functioned as a consulting group to individual brand managers (called Product Sponsors at the company).
The group continues to be dedicated to "promoting a view of unity, coherence and simplicity, and creating clear, effective names."

## COMPARING APPLES...
## TO APRICOTS??

What had happened at IBM had been occurring right across the industry, and right around the world: Unprotected trade marking, leading to potentially successful products lapsing into generic use.

Some computer companies simply "lucked in," if you wish. Whether by good fortune or by conscious design, the name "Apple" has caught on around the world, with its almost-subconscious image of the fruit which purportedly fell upon Issac Newton and gave him his "light bulb" insight into how gravity works. (And how informative that "Newton" is the name of that company's latest portable computing wonder.)

Apple, then, is a name which will last. And at the time of its emergence, that name successfully bucked a powerful trend toward hard-edged, technological names which incorporated all those now-cliché terms which I noted at the start of this chapter: "Comm," "Sys," "Digital," "Tech," and so on. And all those endless, often confusing initials, from "AT&T" to "NCR" to "DEC."

True, the success of Apple drew countless imitators who reached for the fruit bowl as well, but it seems as if only Britain's "Apricot" computers has been able to persist.

174

And poor Japan has only slowly recognized that heavy, old, traditional, clunky, industrial names such as "Mitsubishi" and "Nippon" have come to have distinct disadvantages.

## BUGS IN THE FORBIDDEN FRUIT

To a billion people, Apple--at least in the 1990s--
meant Apple Computers.  But to tens of millions
of more--at least those who were in their teens,
20s, or 30s in the 1960s--Apple was the famous
record company of The Beatles rock group.

The British musical foursome, of course, was the
first to use the name; Apple records begun to
distribute their memorable albums in 1967, a full
decade before two young computer genii named
Steve Jobs and Steve Wozniak joined together to
form Apple computers.

And the Beatles, understandably, registered their
Apple trademark in nearly every country where
their very popular music was sold.

After years of negotiations, the matter was
apparently resolved in 1981, when the computer
firm paid the Beatles an undisclosed sum for the
right to  use the Apple name on personal
computers and related products.  But just three
years later, when the Macintosh computer was
introduced--with its miraculous ability to record
and synthesize sound--the Beatles' firm soon
sought royalties on the trademark in the case of
computers which impinged upon their musical
image.  They could not agree, and in 1989,
Apples Corps sued Apple Computer in England.

The case continued to be fought into the 90s,
showing that, even when agreements are reached,
future technological discoveries can destroy
those resolutions as rapidly as a computer can
compute numbers--or music.  (And not cheaply,
either:
In the second quarter of 1991, Apple Computer
wrote off **$38-million** as a "reserve" of the
lawsuit against it by Apple Corps.)

## SO HOW SHOULD ONE NAME
## A HI-TECH COMPANY, PRODUCT
## OR SERVICE?

What are the lessons in all this?  Lessons which **had better** reach our brains at the speed of light, like our computers supposedly do?

Corporations in this last decade of the 20th century will want their corporate names to convey a modern, socially-responsible, commercial entity.  Hi-tech companies have sadly created a still-pervasive image of too-many-computers, and too-many-layers-of-information; often cumbersome, and with reduced human interaction:

**In other words: "If you wish to reach sales, press ONE"; "If you wish to reach billing, press TWO"; "If you wish to reach a human, just forget it and hang up."**

In the 1990s, modern, fast-growth service companies will undoubtedly wish to convey images of:

SOFT-INFO-MANAGEMENT
rather than a
HARD-WARE-WAREHOUSE
sort of name.

What are some of the problems involved in creating effective names for computers--and for many other modern products and services, for that matter? Let us list some:

One should avoid names which use highly-diluted and over-used words. As noted above, many hi-tech words are dreadfully overused, from "micro" to "info" to "data" to "software" to "control."

Names which are in use today may **not** be available for extended jurisdiction when one's company or product distribution grows.

Also to be eschewed are names which are chosen for personnel, rather than business, reasons. A small, one-man/one-woman firm may wish to name a fledgling company by using kids' first names--Mark and Susan, for instance--to form "Marksue Corp." But one must think of the long-term implications for that business, recalling that nearly all large, international firms began as small businesses, sometime in the past.

Names that are descriptive-only are **not** easily remembered; only the **type** of business, and **not** the product, is remembered by the public! So, names such as Human Designed Systems, or Telecommunication Terminal Systems, or Transaction Management Inc., should be ditched.

Names that are difficult or confusing are quickly forgotten by the consumer.

Kanematsu-Gosho and Nissho Iwai hardly trip off the tongue, probably even in Japan. And the same goes for Standard Memories Trendata.

Over the years, more and more consumer software manufacturers have been increasingly adopting packaged-goods marketing methods. And considering the horrible, daily dilemma of Miss Matilda Johnson in her Grade Two class, and the horrible, daily dilemma of millions of computer purchasers who have suffered through millions of meaningless, forgettable initials and acronyms and gobbledygook--it hasn't been a moment too soon.

# CASE STUDY:

## SHACKS, HUTS, AND TENTS

Several years ago, INTERTAN, responsible
for a couple of thousand Radio Shack consumer
electronic stores world-wide, called me for a
meeting in Belgium.

All their international managers were present;
clearly this was a major project! For six hours
everyone discussed the pros and cons of the
buying habits of the world public, the perception
of electronic names--even Radio Shack's itself,
their competitors, and the impact of the upsurge
of electronic names, as well as upcoming
products.

The next few meetings led to the development
of the name **GENEXXA.** This name is a
hi-tech brand of new products which reflect
cutting edge technologies. Today, some 1,000
products are being marketed under this name.
Radio Shack would remain a middle of the road
supplier of general consumer electronics.

The original name of the company, of course,
is widely known, and equally problematical:
The word "shack" is a 1940s term, which is more
appropriate for a dusty barn in a No Man's Land,
providing the **least** reliable service. Even worse,
the name is primarily driven as a discounted
supplier of unwanted items.

And so, companies, **despite** an often successful
bottom line, sometimes struggle with their
names, as seen earlier in the Honeywell/Bull
story. "Shack" is a strongly American word,
and is not generally understood outside the
continental U.S.

This has led to many customers, in various
countries around the world, to write to
"Mr. Shack," complaining of a radio not
working, since it is perceived as a man's name!
As you can see, what had become a
highly dated image in the United States,
was seen as a fairly interesting family name
in several other countries.

"Shack," furthermore, is a slang term in the U.S.,
while a word like "Hut" is understood more
widely. As one can see, names can certainly
prove to be problems, even decades after
they are chosen!

In the case of the name Pizza Hut, which is
a rather acceptable name in North America,
because we don't live in huts, it is a **terrible**
name around the world because it conveys
the negative meaning of the word "hut,"
which is understood in hundreds of dialects
as a filthy, dirty, unhygenic slum-like dwelling.

A place to reside in when poor, but when you
can afford it, definitely not a place to go out
to eat.

## THE FUTURE OF HI-TECH NAMING

The casualness of the '80s, which provided the most challenging, provocative backbone of the computer industry, out of Silicon Valley, should not be turned immediately into the likes of undertakers and Wall Street bankers. It requires a more sensible and **reliable** nomenclature for the general public to really understand what they are getting with their computer and all other hi-tech products.

Like many other industries, the computer industry has matured--although in a far shorter time period. Now, however, after many years of confusion, it must **demonstrate** that maturity by having proper corporate and product identification standards and correct nomenclature.

**The end-user has become confused by names which are still being thrown at it like a runaway ticker tape.**

We must look at the literal explosion of human interphase with computerization in our times. Computerization has become actual extension of our own bodies.

And never before, in the ten thousand years of recorded history, have we human beings been **so** accessible to an inter-cultural society!

# CASE STUDY:

## ACCOUNTING FOR A NEW NAME

The North American sector of the international consulting firm of KPMG had acquired a C.A.S.E. (Computer Aided Software Engineering) product, consisting of computer-aided software, for its global market, which includes over 5,000 offices and affiliates worldwide. It needed a name, of course.

The goal of the name, in this case, was **not only** for masses to interact with, but its many employees as well. Of course, the explosion of hi-tech names over the past few decades added greatly to the difficulty of my job.

We were given a strong mandate by the CEO to look for a cutting-edge name, and we were fortunate to have a very bright and gung-ho accountants who participated in the process.

Naturally, all of their internal naming groups had collapsed, prior to my arrival, and the problems were complex:

Here was a corporation that would sell a C.A.S.E. product, and one which was divided into two distinct stages of application; a front end system, and a back end system.

Some kind of umbrella name was necessary, but one which also had to stand on two pillars, which imposed phenomenally difficult demands. For instance, one did not wish to call it something like TREES, and then FLOWERS; then the fourth or fifth generation of products would run into further naming problems, FRUITS and FRUITFLIES.

After several briefings and presentations, we applied a corporate name for the $100,000 software product: **ZEROTIME.** It was a good name, and for numerous reasons: "Zero" is a word understood in some 100 countries and several hundred languages; the word "Time" is understood equally widely.

Furthermore, the name could be quickly registered, and protected in 80 countries around the globe. Not surprisingly, ZEROTIME took off. And what of the "front-end" and "back-end" sub-products? Here we had been inspired by the images of goldfish and silverfish, and our final decision was **GOLDRUN** and **SILVERRUN**. (After all, computers do not walk, do they? But they do **run!**)

With GOLDRUN and SILVERRUN, the modulation concept was captured. And furthermore, both words fit in well with the umbrella name, ZEROTIME.

From start to finish, the project took six weeks. And it is firmly imprinted in my memory, because a TV crew from the Canadian Broadcasting Corporation chose to attend all of the meeting, both at our offices, and at the rooms of KPMG.  It was eventually broadcast on the internationally-respected business show VENTURE, with the total amount of time allotted to this "naming segment" being exactly half of the show--**hardly** ZEROTIME! And, although this program was televised over five years ago, I am still asked about it.

Today, GOLDRUN and SILVERRUN are successful C.A.S.E. products all over the world.

*The electronic world has made it possible for us to live, almost simultaneously, around the globe, in over 100 countries and over 1,000 languages and dialects. No longer can a new technology product, service, or corporation call itself something silly, and be understood and respected around the planet.*

# Novo-Consumerism

# 10

Many businesses
believe that
consumers are
simply sheep.
But they had better
beware:  Consumers
are rapidly becoming
wolves in sheep's
clothing.

**P**ut aside your can of
Coke or Pepsi for a
moment, if you don't
mind, and take a look
at the following "brand names":
Marlboro. Coca-Cola. Intel.
Kellogg. Nescafe. Budweiser.
Pepsi. Gillette. Pampers.
Bacardi.

What do they all have in common? If you
happened to see that major study of
internationally-known products conducted by
**Financial World** magazine and published in
the summer of 1993, you'll surely remember:
They make up the top ten "most valuable
brands," which suggests, in the words of the
magazine, that the threat from "private/store
label" products is **not** as widespread as brand
manufacturers originally feared.

The numbers attached to those names are mind-boggling, by the way. The name "Marlboro" is apparently worth just under **$40-billion** to cigarette manufacturer Philip Morris Company; Coca-Cola is estimated as having a value of a similarly-towering $33-billion-plus; Intel, nearly $18-billion; the rest of the top ten range from nearly $10-billion (Kellogg), down to Bacardi Rum's still awesome $5.5-billion in value. Even a number as low as 58th on **Financial World's** list of "world's richest brands," Tropicana orange juice, still rang in at a tidy $1-billion.

Let's look at Marlboro alone for a moment, and its purported value. According to **Forbes** magazine, Marlboro accounted for 28% of Philip Morris's $25-billion in revenue in 1986, and brought in **over one-half** of its operating profits - - or $2-billion. In fact, Marlboro averaged more than 3% growth in the U.S., at a time when the industry had shrunk up to 2% a year in unit sales. And as for international sales--and the power of brand names, a German-born architect was quoted in **Forbes** in 1987 as saying, "If Americans want to be chic like a European, they have to buy a Mercedes or BMW. For us, it is easier; all we have to do is smoke Marlboros and wear jeans."

**Clearly, having a internationally-recognized brand name is like money in the bank.**

**Or is it?**

## WHAT ABOUT THOSE "STORE BRANDS"?

Let's shift now to a **different** set of names, as you gently push your No-name cola away from this book, and take a look at these names.

**President's Choice**
**Master's Choice**
**Sam's Choice**
**People's Choice**
**HealthyChoice**
**Your Choice**
**My Choice**

Not terribly impressive at first glance, are they? I'm talking here about so-called store brands, of course, whose effect on those above-mentioned, internationally-renowned brand names has been close to shocking, over the past few years--to the point of panic price-cutting and wholesale firings. (The August 23,1993 issue of **Fortune** reminds us of Proctor & Gamble's recent "expunging" of **one-fourth** of its "myriad shapes and sizes of products, and its plans to close 20% of its factories around the world, and cut 13,000 jobs"--**12%** of its total number of employees. If they had **their** choice (whether President's or Master's or Sam's), would these newly unemployed P&G workers want to **strangle** the producers of store brand products with their bare, generic hands?

Obviously, private label products have come a long way since the 1980s, when no-name generic products, often wrapped in ugly yellow and white packaging, made us feel like apple-sellers during the Great Depression when we reached for them on the shelf.

A **very** long way.  Just a few short years ago, nationally-known brand names, like the top ten listed in the marginalia, above, could be trusted to be significantly superior to those hideously-unattractive, cheaply-packaged generic ones, often (humorously) called No-Name This and No-Name That.

And, also only yesterday, shoppers who turned to those cheaper store brands could be trusted to **return** to their beloved brand names, the very second that  hubby got his job back, or the Ms. got a promotion.  True, things like generic, No-Name paper plates and eggs and very standardized dairy products continue to thrive, even in Good Times, but **something quite extraordinary has happened.**  To quote the CEO of Wal-Mart Stores in the United States, David Glass, "Things are really changing. There's a tremendous amount of quality in private label."

Quality is only half of it.  These no-name products often continue to cost between **15% and 40% less** than the Cokes and Pampers of the world, and you **don't** have to be unemployed, under-employed or even lower-middle-class to want to save a few pennies here and there.

### GATORADE

Percentage of the sports-drink field held by Gatorade: **90%**

Amount of money spent on sports drinks: **$500-million**

Name of Coca-Cola's 1990 entry up against Quaker Oat's Gatorade Brand: **PowerAde**

Name of PepsiCo's new Gatorade knockoff: **Mountain Dew Sport**

Why, even the very rich are often quite proud to put a non-brand name product on their tablecloth-covered, elaborately-set dining room table; there are some pretty interesting "choices" now being offered with that purportedly **non**-brand name on the box.

Indeed, several major "once No-Name" products have, in fact, become the latest, major "brand names," due to massive advertising campaigns, store shelf space, and word-of-mouth. (Not unlike a small business which quite suddenly, through financial success, has turned into a big business.  More on this, below.)

True, this all pales next to 1776 in the U.S. and 1789 in France, but there **is** a revolution going on, and the importance of brand names and their centrality to the market place has been shaken to the core in recent years.

As one Canadian newspaper put it, "Store brands . . . have evolved in the past decade **from imitator to innovator** [emphasis mine]; from appealing mainly to price-conscious consumers, to attracting a broad cross-section of customers; from seeking a niche market to competing head-to-head with some formidable national brands."

You bet your Gillette they have.  Here are just a few highlights (or "low lights," if you happen to own stock in Heinz, Colgate-Palmolive, or Dell Computer):

President's Choice Decadent Chocolate Chip Cookie has been the best-selling cookie in Canada for the past two years, even though it is sold in but **one of five** stores across the country!

"Store brands" have risen to 18% of **all** supermarket sales volume in the United States.

**Store brand soft drinks actually outsold Coke and Pepsi** in Ontario supermarkets during the months of April and May, 1993. (And just **wait** until a wildly-successful Canadian private-label bottler called Cott's has its cola drinks for Wal-Mart's stores really catch on, in the U.S.)

Saks Fifth Avenue has hit $63-million a year with its three "private labels" for women, which now represents 20% of that chain's women's sportswear business.

President's Choice Szechwan Peanut Sauce outsells all brands of ketchup in many of its Loblaws stores in Canada--even, yes, Heinz ketchup, the one which you always expected to find in the finest restaurants and homes.

Here's the real killer: In Loblaws' chain of No-Frill stores (where you've got to bag it yourself, and even bring your own boxes or bags), both their No-Name and President's Choice products currently make up approximately **two-thirds** of all sales.

## HEARTBREAKS

You gotta have heart, but can't use it in U.S. ads.

Canbra Foods Ltd. of Alberta spent over $5-million to launch a major product for the U.S. market called Heartlight salad oil, so-named because it is made from the healthful canola seed.

After 2-and-a-half years in the market, the firm was notified by the U.S. Food and Drug Administration that they had six months to **change** the brand name: Companies were no longer allowed to use heart" (or "fresh", "healthy" or "new") in their brand names.

As Bob Dylan sang a quarter century ago, "Something's happening/but you don't know what it is/Do you Mr. Jones?"  And the fact has been proven, in the past few months alone, by Philip Morris slashing the price of Marlboros by 40 cents, and by the top two dozen manufacturers of internationally-recognized brand name products starting to lose close to $50-billion in market value over the second quarter of 1993. Prudential Securities keeps track of well-known name brand food stocks on the NYSE; during the summer of 93, these shares were selling at 22% discount to the Standard & Poor industrials, making their lousiest showing in over a decade. (Well, Mr. Jones?)

The question is, does it mean that brand names have lost their seemingly-inherent value. (**Value?**  How about Nescafe's name being worth $9.2-billion, and Nike's being worth $3.5-billion?)

Or should the question really go like this:  **In a time of continual recessionary cycles, is not a brand name, or a thoughtfully-chosen, highly-creative "new" name, all the more important, as (purportedly) "generic names" cut savagely into their market share?**

Certainly,  President's Choice products are no longer **truly** cheap, and markedly inferior, as they were only a few years ago in their unpleasant yellow  configuration.

**In point of fact, "President's Choice" is really no longer a generic product at all, but rather a well-priced, good-value brand name, and the result of inspired marketing (at an opportune time)--along with a then-original "choice" of name. Pun intended, and not apologized for.**

## WHAT ABOUT STORE LABEL FASHIONS?

Let's look at the much-talked-about Return of the Store Label in fashion for a moment. Back in the boom years of the post-war 1950s in America, before designers turned into Madonna-like superstars, shoppers were happy to buy "store labels." Women were delighted--and proud--to wear a skirt or dress with "Bergdorf Goodman" or "Saks Fifth Avenue" sewn carefully on the inside of the collar or waist.

Today, as we have seen so far in this chapter, shoppers have become more price-conscious than ever, and stores have begun to create store labels once again.

From Barneys New York to J.C. Penny right across the United States, women's clothes are being manufactured, and sold, and **expensively promoted**, under their own store labels.

Not unlike the way Wal-Mart in the U.S. has accepted Cott's offer from Canada to create a store brand/private label called Sam's Choice for its many thousands of stores, clothing chains have chosen to eliminate the designer (in other words, "by-pass Coke and Pepsi"), which frees them to sell their clothes for much **less**, and still make **more** profit from them.

## THE LICENSING OF BRAND NAMES

Sales of licensed products with designer names and logos from such brands as Coca-Cola and Greyhound in 1986: **$19-billion.** Sales with cartoon characters, such as those of Walt Disney: **$12.5-billion.** Toys and games-licensed products: **$8.3-billion.** Total of licensed products sold in 1986: **$54-billion.** Increase from 1983: **66%.**

But while many private-label items have been a boon to consumers (since who doesn't love "getting a deal" on something?), and given retailers a competitive edge, they have also created real difficulties for many manufacturers of goods, household products and clothes. After all, many of these companies find themselves in the awkward position of selling goods to stores which have now become their **competitors**! Furthermore, several of these manufacturers are **also** making the private label products for those stores, which can mean that **their own name brands can be squeezed off the shelves.** So the "one man's meat is another man's poison" cliché seems to have some truth in it, in the world of brand names and private labels.

**Furthermore, the risk can be even greater, if great names are not carefully chosen for products, whether so-called brand labelled ones, or new, private labels!** Every now and then, I encounter a name development exercise in the world of fashion, and I know from the very outset that it is doomed to failure. It is a painful and even cruel exercise to watch (supposed) grown-up men and women running around in circles, having put no strategic value on the process of name choice.

Here is one example: I was once rushed into an office, along with several others, to review a list of some 500 (!) names for fashion label "ladies' apparel" for a very large, well-established and esteemed department store chain.

The agency involved insisted that we produce our evaluation, and a summary of those 500 names, within the same day. (**Within the same day? To paraphrase a famous airline commercial, "Is this any way to run a business?"**)

These strange and questionable names had been developed internally (see Chapter II!) in conjunction with their agency, the marketing department of the company, and several focus groups (see Chapter II **again**!) The five hundred names on the list consisted of such dubious monikers as "Sabina." And "Sabrina." And "Sabrina Plus." And "LaSabina." Ad nauseum.

Try to say these names quickly--or even try to say them **at all**--and you might be putting your vocal cords at risk. But then, this what happens when one works with one's marketing department and focus groups to come up with names that are expected to make or break a product. Or a **company**, for that matter.

In fact, that is precisely what happened: A major department store chain ended up being severely damaged because of this lack of sensitivity and thoughtfulness, in the creation of an important fashion label for their clothing.

Here is what transpired: When our research was
done by the end of the day, we had only seven
names left. The names were unique, to be sure;
but they were odd, too: Ones such as
"Jean Paul Vincent," and "Guy-Paul Sebastien,"
and others of that ilk.

The problems were immediately evident, at least
to this man: All seven names had serious
difficulties with either the spelling and/or the
pronunciation, and none of them were clearly
available in both Canada and the United States.

The end result--because of the panic involved in
this last minute crash course in fashion label
naming--was just what you may have guessed:
No name was adopted.

But that's not **all**. This important department
store chain, with many dozens of stores across
the continent, closed down its entire business in
1991. Several thousand men and women lost
their jobs, and a century-old tradition of retailing
had come to a crashing end.

**Nor is this case atypical.** In a sadly similar
situation, I once sat at another meeting with
senior merchandising vice presidents of a
department chain corporation which had been in
operation for nearly two centuries. At this
meeting, it was declared in no uncertain terms by
almost everyone present that "names are not
important to invest any time in." This is hardly
the way for responsible brand managers to think!

This group of very important VPs had a clear understanding amongst themselves that they could pick any name that they liked, from anywhere in North America, and start using it. Then, they actually admitted, **if and when they received any legal objection by an original creator, they would pretend it was a genuine mistake.** And this was the way they had been running their entire fashion label merchandising section, which consisted of several floors of a major high-rise in an urban setting.

Once again, no big surprise here: A few years later, as part of a major layoff of several thousand employees, this **entire** building was eliminated--which included, of course, the three floors of the fashion label management which had shown so little respect for the power and impact of names.

Can the demise of these two major clothing firms (or key portions thereof) be laid directly at the feet of their absurdly naive, even infantile, attitude toward the importance of names? Perhaps not entirely. But I believe that there is very little question that their respective attitudes toward naming must have had some significant influence upon the process of their mutual failures in the marketplace.

Not everyone in the fashion industry acts as unprofessionally as those two examples I've just shared. As noted earlier, more and more major stores have woken up to the importance of private fashion labels.

Not unlike the truly inspired actions of
Dave Nichol and his President's Choice brands of
food-and-related products, an increasing number
of retailers have gone this route, and with far
greater wisdom. Just as President's Choice has
turned to quality, and a vast, often highly-
creative and original group of consumer
products, so have these fashion retailers. And as
both quality and fashionability have improved
dramatically, private store labels have been
taking on much greater importance for the
Bergdorf Goodmans, Saks, Barneys and Penny's
of the world.

As the **New York Times** noted in the summer of
1993, "To get the customer to buy private label, it
has to be something special, not just a navy
jacket." (And in the case of so-called "private
labellers" in the grocery store world, offering
such exotic things as "President's Choice
Szechwan Peanut Sauce" amounts to much the
same attitude.) Also, with a private store label
with fashions, just as with those food store
private labels, one can control one's business
better. As one major merchandise manager for
the women's store of Barneys New York--
using the catchy name of Barneys New York
Collection, which was initiated in 1986 and now
accountes for **fully one-half of its sales**--
declares, "With a designer-name collection, you
can't control deliveries and you have to mark
down the clothes when other stores do." But
when the clothes have your **own** name on them,
you can.

## BRAND NAMES: WORTH FIGHTING FOR?

Which brings us back to the so-called "Store-brand Revolution." (As **Fortune Magazine**'s sub-title of a major article on this subject read in August, 1993, "Private-label makers and their retailer conspirators are putting tremendous pressure on big brands. Famous names are fighting back. This battle is far from over.")

And it's going to be one helluva battle. For one thing, consumers who fear for their jobs and the roof over their heads might start questioning how much of that $2.50 they paid in the ball park for a soft drink went to pay the million-dollar-plus salary of Michael J. Fox or Michael Jackson.

As one major retailer of no-name products was recently quoted as complaining, "Advertising as practiced in industries like beer and soft drinks is one of the greatest economic wastes in our society. I question their strategy of using superstars. I think they might be harming themselves . . . I think there is going to be a consumer rebellion to all the advertising expenses of the major North American retailers, and it could be the downfall of the great branded companies."

**LAUNCHING NEW PRODUCTS**

Cost of launching a new product in

1975: $10-million
1986: $100-million
1994: $150-million

Cost of buying a company which owns a major, established brand name: Varies.

Not so fast, Mr. No-Name. **One must never underestimate the power of classic brand names, and the impact which they continue to have on consumers**--even if they cringe when they hear of $20-million going to Michael Jackson for dancing with a Pepsi can.

The fact remains:  A leading brand is a lot like a thriving oil well;  it will earn a good cash flow. A major brand can still command price premiums of up to 20% over its less-well-known competitors.  Although there be limits to that premium, especially in hard times.  In the October 18, 1993 **New York Times**, the departing president of the trade organization representing giant advertisers warned, "I don't have any questions whatsoever about the power of brands, but many manufacturers have escalated retail prices beyond the value that the consumer perceives to be in their brands."

The indisputable **difference** from that oil well is, a brand name <u>never</u> stops gushing huge profits. **Of the top brands in North America in 1925, 18 of them are still the number-one brand in their categories, nearly seven decades later!** And no amount of wildly-successful private labels can deny that historically-proven fact.

You may recognize some of them:  Eveready
Batteries;  Kellogg's breakfast cereals; Ivory
Soap; Goodyear Tires; Del Monte canned fruit;
Crisco Shortening; Sherwin-Williams Paint;
Wrigley's chewing gum; Campbell's Soup;
Kodak Film; Lipton Tea, and several more.
And you don't even have to **ask** for Coca-Cola;
it's already been poured for you.

Nor can the recent success of private labels deny
the traditional impact of classic brand names on
the stock markets of the world:  Between 1985
and 1988, for example, the share price of a
sample of "brand-heavy" companies rose **over
66%**.  Yet Standard & Poor's 500 average
was up just **3%** during those same years.

As one prominent journalist wrote on the power
of brand names in the late '80s, "Overwhelmed
by choice, dogged by doubts of new and
unfamiliar names, [consumers] reach almost
inevitably for the old faithfuls on the top shelf.
And as long as that's so, owning the right names
will be the most solid security of all."

In the world of toys, to give a playful example
for a moment, the power and value of established
names **also** play a ferociously important role.  In
1985, for example, five items accounted for
around $1.5 billion in revenues, or almost
one-fifth of the entire industry that year.

You may remember some of them, too,
depending on the ages of your children:

- TONKA'S GOBOTS
- KENNER-PARKER'S CARE BEARS
- HASBRO'S TRANSFORMERS
- MATTEL'S MASTERS OF THE UNIVERSE
- COLECO'S CABBAGE PATCH KIDS

That's a lot of Christmas-tree fertilizing.

And as for the differences between the sexes
(as well as brands), take a look at this: Hasbro's
G.I. Joe line of action toys climbed in sales from
$50-million in 1982 to $136-million, only three
years later. And Barbie dolls continue to sell in
the hundreds of millions of dollars every single
year for Mattel. (Allowing Barbie's mummy-
company to purchase Fisher-Price for over a
billion dollars in 1993; and if the latter's name
didn't carry such powerful images of
"educational" and "quality," I sense that it
wouldn't have fetched one-tenth that price for the
firm.) But then, recognizable names, whether of
companies or products, always--**always**--add
spectacular value to corporations, whether their
bottom line or the value of their stocks.

## GREAT BRAND NAMES:
## WORTH THEIR WEIGHT IN GOLD --
## SO CHOOSE CAREFULLY!

The almost inestimable value of classic brand names can be captured in a brief, rather strange quote, tossed off in a 1986 article which appeared in **Time**: "There is a perceived way of life embedded in each bottle of Coke. Coke is modern; **with** it." (That was spoken by one Charles Kasinga, of the Kenya office of McCann Erickson. True, he was an executive in charge of the Coca-Cola account in that African country, but that does **not** deny that he knew whereof he spoke.

I highly doubt if Sam's Choice private-label colas will **ever** carry such profound, deeper meaning outside of continental North America.)

And it is not only in Africa where famous brand names capture the allegiance of foreign citizens-- and even symbolize America itself. In 1986, shortly after the United States bombed Libya, a mob in Barcelona stoned a local McDonald's. And the year before, Marxists in Peru sprayed graffiti and burned tables at three of Lima's five Kentucky Fried Chicken restaurants. What better statements (even if violent, anti-American ones) about the power, the meaning, the sense of world-domination by famous-brand consumer products, than in those two actions in Western Europe and South America?

Those mobs certainly knew what brands represented the United States!  Symbolism aside, how about the **value** of brand names to the companies which are fortunate enough to own them?  In 1988, the British conglomerate Grand Metropolitan announced something quite extraordinary:  That it would give value in its balance sheet to some of its better known brand names, such as J B Rare Scotch and Bailey's Irish Cream.  The company decided to publish just one single figure for the value of all its brands, and did not attempt to value them individually.  This move added approximately 500 million pounds to the worth of the then 4.5-billion pound company.

Nor need we limit ourselves only to our cousins in the Old Country.  As **Newsweek** noted in 1985,  "Brand names have clout with consumers who now, more than ever, know a good quality buy when they see it.  They are immune from foreign competition and are big profit centers.  At P&G, for example, six products (CREST, CHEER, DOWNY, TIDE, PAMPERS, and LUVS) account for more than 50 percent of the profits. . . . "

"No. 1 brand names are more important than market share in the long term," declared one prominent business school professor, "They are more valuable now then they've been since the '50s."  True, that may have appeared in print nearly a decade ago, but the passing years, and the increase in so-called private labels, do not give the lie to those words.

## DON'T FIGHT THEM--BUY THEM!!

Indeed, one major reason for the burst of
acquisitions of consumer-goods companies in the
1980s (Philip Morris swallowing General Foods
for $5.8-billion; P&G paying $1.2-billion in cash
for Richardson-Vicks, of Nyquil, Oil of Olay and
Vidal Sassoon shampoo fame) was simple:
**It's easier to buy someone else's well-
established brand name than it is to (try and)
create one's own.** Manufacturers spend upwards
of $80-million to launch a new product, while
four-fifths of all new products fail. So, why on
earth should P&G have spent over a decade
(and tens of millions) to establish its Wondra
skin lotion as a wonder; by purchasing
Richardson-Vicks, it suddenly found itself
**the owner** of the best-selling lotion in the
world: Oil of Olay. Pretty smart, eh?

So it was not by chance when, in the fall of 1988,
RJR Nabisco's proud gathering of brand names
(from Animal Crackers for the kids to Winston
cigarettes for the parents) was sold for
$25-billion, it nearly doubled what had ever
before been paid for a single company. As
**The Economist** of England noted at the time,
"Brands used to defeat rustlers. Today, they
mesmerize hustlers. . . . The advertising jingles
that people hum, and the names (Hoover, Perrier,
Xerox, Coke) they seize upon as shorthand for
everyday things, seem to translate into ever-
larger billions."
**You bet they do.**

The need to recognize the value of internationally-known brand names is constantly coming up in the news, and has often cost companies and their shareholders many millions of dollars. One example which will live in infamy was the way Rowntree of York, England, showed net assets of only 408.6 million pounds for its company (which includes such names as Kit Kat and Quality Street) in its 1987 annual report. Nestle, however, could smell their value, and offered **more than six times the book value of Rowntree's assets** in a takeover bid in the summer of 1988. And only the year before, Grand Metropolitan bought Smirnoff, the world-famous vodka producer, for $1.2-billion, and found that it had to write-off two-thirds of that as "goodwill." As **The Economist** noted with some dismay, "It might have avoided this if it had attached a value to the Smirnoff name."

Indeed, if all companies attached more value to their names, and the names of their products, this book would not be necessary.

In recent years, there has been a growing awareness that, as a brand name goes, so goes the firm which holds it or manufacturers it. So, for instance, the Canadian department store chain T. Eaton recently announced that it would not only continue to plug the many products it sells, but also stress the benefits of simply shopping **there**.

As their PR manager noted, "We want to let customers know that we've got it all under one roof--the products, the service and the after-service."

Underlining this awareness was a survey of over 2,700 American, Canadian and European businesses, which showed that "firms whose brands lead their categories earn an average return of investment of 31%, and companies whose brands actually **dominate** their markets earn 34% on average." True, if one's brands are barely hanging on to the top spot--"marginal leaders," they are called--the average return on investment drops to 26%. But that's still **well** above the 21% average return on investment earned by those firms whose brands are in second place within any given category, or the 16% return for third-ranking brands, or the 12% return earned by those whose brands are in fourth place or lower.

To put this crucial statistic into a single sentence: **Companies whose brands are dominant in their categories are 52% more profitable than their nearest competitors!** And you wondered why RJR Nabisco was tossing billions around to lasso some famous brand names?

In another survey done in 1991, in which some 2,000 people aged 15 and older were asked about the "perceived value" or brand "equity" of nearly 200 famous brand names, consumers reported that the ones with the highest perceived quality were "wholesome, nurturing, and caring."

Furthermore, the **brand names with that "high" perception sold at more than three times the rate of brands rated as "quite" acceptable in quality.**

In this major study, the top ten brands radiating such value/equity were Disney World/Disney Land, Kodak, Mercedes-Benz, CNN, Hallmark, Fisher-Price, UPS, Rolex, Levi's, and IBM.

Of course, every one of those brand names are both known, and respected, around the globe. And, recalling the attacks on McDonald's restaurants in Europe in anti-American frenzy, let us never forget the **flip-side** of that hatred: The acceptance, and even passionate longing, for anything and everything which hints of America, from its freedoms to its wealth to its-- yes, to its brand name products.

It is noteworthy to mention that at the Beijing Yansha, the first department store in the People's Republic of China which opened in the summer of 1992, the growing number of wealthy Chinese were irresistibility draw to internationally-known brand names.

One of the store's best-selling areas is devoted entirely to Nike athletic shoes and sportswear.

A textile worker was interviewed there by the **Washington Post,** which discovered that she was about to purchase a pair of Nike high-top sneakers for about $39 U.S., which was nearly equal to her monthly income. "You can't find shoes like this in Beijing," she told the reporter. "I only wear brand names, and I like these shoes, so it's okay to spend more if I like them."

And that's a market of 1.2 billion, which could someday have a **lot** of disposable income.

*We live in a post-CNN, 500 channel, media-junkie society. Whether we live in Utah or the Ukraine, we know what is going on from Fifth Avenue to Rodeo Drive, from Ginza to Via Roma. To assume that today's consumers can be fooled by inferior products being sold as premium brands is fatal.*

# Custody of a Name

# 11

Why would anyone want to share their valued brand name with their competitors and others? Why not have 100% custody of the name, so it can be nurtured to maturity?

 *look through any trade directory will show dozens, sometimes even hundreds of businesses, products, and services, often with identical names, competing for the same turf. This creates a legal frenzy for lawyers, and a ludicrous waste of marketing and advertising dollars.*

Of course, Nike did not get into China, and a hundred other countries, without protecting and registering its now-billion-dollar brand name. The **Wall Street Journal** noted in 1988 that it's getting more and more costly to avoid litigation over trademarks. Six-figure settlements to acquire the rights to previously registered trademarks became everyday occurrences over the past few years, and with good reason.

"Little-known brand names suddenly become very valuable when companies find out we may be interested in the same names," a VP at Stroh Brewery Co. of Detroit declared. (His firm had to pay hefty amounts to a number of other companies for the right to use brand names for its new non-alcoholic beverages, High Five and Sundance.)

A similar occurrence took place between two major companies, Mennen and Revlon. When the latter chose the name "Trouble" for a new fragrance for women, it was shocked to discover that Mennen was already using that name for a men's cologne in Central America. Revlon ended up paying a large amount of cash for the right to use the name, and limit Mennen's name on its cologne to only certain countries.

The President of Revlon's cosmetics and fragrances group, Arne Zimmerman, noted soon after, "What good is a successful perfume if we can't go world-wide with it?" I agree.

A new trademark law was passed by the Congress of the United States in October of 1988, which eased the agony of creating a good brand name a bit, while increasing the pain of those who already succeeded: The new law allowed a company to register its trademark for 10 years, exactly half of the earlier 20 years for which they could be protected.

And if it wished to renew its trademark registration, any company had to prove it was actively **using** the name, and not just holding it in reserve.

## COST OF A GOOD NAME

Amount of money paid by Canadian-based billion-dollar software developer SHL Systemhouse Inc., when it bought **ComputerLand** Canada Inc. from its U.S. parent in 1988 "for the right to use the ComputerLand name":

$40.5-million

217

## CHINESE TRADEMARKS

By the end of 1985, China had registered 3,816 trademarks, of which 1,194 were registered in over **100** foreign countries.

Today, Far Eastern businesses are **the** most active players in the global trademarking game.

And so, the litigations continue. In 1987, General Mills lost a major battle against International Yogurt Co. over the national rights to the name "YoCreme," and was forced to stop making its own yogurt product of the same name. Part of the final settlement entailed General Mills paying nearly a quarter of a million dollars to International Yogurt, which had been selling-- and continues to sell--YoCreme frozen Yogurt. (And we **warned** them to check the phone books carefully!)

Not that looking in a phone book keeps the predators away! Several years ago, an enterprising Australian businessman saw the name Budget Rent A Car (a trademark registered in many countries around the world, **including** Down Under) , and began to call his own car rental business "Budget." His argument was that "budget" **is** a word in common usage, and not distinctive of any one company's business, in spite of its world-wide use by the American firm.

The high court of Australia did not agree, and ruled that "A name composed of descriptive words is capable of becoming distinctive of a particular business." The Australian entrepreneur was forced to take the name "Budget" off his store and automobiles.

But just how far should this protection of "brand names" go?

## THE RINGS OF FIRE

At least twenty-five times a century, struggles
over the Olympic name erupt like a volcano.
And by the time the Olympic memorabilia hit the
local flea markets, the lava is ready to flow again.

The enthusiastic desire of the Olympic
Committee lawyers to go after fry -- no matter
how small -- to protect their precious name is
fully understandable.

Yet it is also not easy.  As the "Olympic Issue" of
**Sports Illustrated** asked in a hilarious article in
the fall of 1988, "Is there any fair-sized town that
does not have an Olympic Diner somewhere on
its outskirts?  One Olympic Diner leads into two
Olympic Realty offices, which lead into three
Olympic Laundromats.  There seem to be no
boundaries.  These Olympics are everywhere.
Around the country.  Around the world.  The
Olympic Diner of Abu Dhabi?  The Olympic
Diner of  Beijing?  The Olympic Diner of
Moscow?  Everywhere."

Indeed, the Manhattan telephone book lists 58
Olympic numbers; the Chicago one has 33; the
downtown Los Angeles directory has 137--and
with very good reason; the games have been held
there twice, and there's an Olympic Boulevard in
the city, making even **more** stores with that name
inevitable.

## CHINA ADVERTISING

Number of companies which advertised in the People's Republic of China in 1982: **100**

Number which advertised by 1984: **4,000**

Amount by which advertising increased since 1979 per year: **50%**

Better get out your Chinese-English dictionaries!

True, your tiny neighborhood Greek restaurant-- as justifiably named "Olympic" as your neighborhood French store has the right to put a drawing of La Tour Eiffel on its matchboxes-- should remain untouched.  But when the organizers of the "Gay Olympic Games" saw their name struck down by the U.S. Supreme Court in 1987,  upholding a 1950 Congressional law which gave the exclusive word to the U.S. Olympic Committee, one can see that the U.S.O.C. meant business.  (And **less** business for those who dare to use the word "Olympic" without licensing it first!)

## REACHING FOR THE STARS

Of course, the search for new names, which every company hopes and even expects will become a magical, internationally-recognized brand name on the level of Coke or Marlboro, can be frustrating, **even when legally protected.** For example, having  an internationally-recognized "brand name" of a movie star would **seem** to be a guarantee of success for a product which has such an honor bestowed upon it.  But this was not always the case.  Cher's Uninhibited perfume dropped from an impressive $15-million in sales in 1988 down to $10-million the very next year, and it was soon for sale (this time, by the company who made it ).  The same for Joan Collins' Spectacular, which did poorly.

As did Julio Iglesias' Only, Mikhail Baryshnikov's Misha, and Herb Alpert's Listen, all of which had been introduced into the crowded, $150-million celebrity perfume and cologne market in the last two years of the previous decade.  Like Coca-Cola or Mercedes-Benz, a movie star's name **can** create immediate (and loving) recognition.  And the success of Elizabeth Taylor's Passion perfume (and a later spin-off, Passion for Men), generated sales of over $65-million in 1989.  But just as a company name can pick up negative connotations (think of EXXON, after the oil-spill disaster in Alaska) , so can an entertainer.  As **Forbes** noted in 1990, "handcuff a perfume to the wrong--for whatever complex, subliminal reasons--image, and the whole campaign stalls.  Not every women wants to associate the way that she smells with the chain-mailed actress [Cher] or a male ballet star [Baryshnikov]."

Cosmetic industry either goes for a soft, invisible message or sometimes for a solid weight dropping on your head.
Products on the market today are:

- FAHRENHEIT

- CELSIUS

- DEGREE

- 360

- GRAVITY

**LETTER FROM E.I. DU PONT TO THE ECONOMIST:**
Sir--Your recent article...about President Reagan, "The Teflon begins to peel?", fails to acknowledge that Teflon is a Du Pont trademark. Teflon should only be used to modify a proper generic.... While these points may appear minor, we feel sure that you will understand Du Pont...invested considerable effort and expense in establishing...its Teflon trademark. If we were to allow the trademark to be used as a generically descriptive word, we would be in danger of losing this valuable property right.

**A.M. Kowalewski**

**THE GLORIOUS SPIN-OFF VALUE OF RECOGNIZABLE BRAND NAMES**

But then there is the very valuable flip-side to using famous names to sell the products on which they are printed. Some brand names are so powerful, they lend themselves to a wide variety of **other** products. For instance, Coca-Cola stunned the world when it refreshed the clothing industry as much as it did its imbibers: Murjani International sold some $200-million worth of clothes emblazoned with the Coca-Cola logo in 1987, alone.

It may all be tracked back to the first Mickey Mouse watch in 1933, but there has been a veritable explosion of "logos" on other products than the ones we normally associate them with. As early as 1985, retailers had sold over **$40-billion worth** of these kinds of goods, ranging from Coca-Cola-emblazoned radios and baseball bats to Harley-Davidson beach towels; from Hershey overalls to Budweiser dart boards and Frisbees. As one sociologist at Columbia University's business school noted, "Wearing these items is a way of broadcasting your preferences to the world." And these "preferences," invariably, are world-renowned brand names.

Note this paragraph from a major news magazine: "Like many companies, Harley-Davidson started licensing its name partly to protect the reputation of its trademark.

Shady operators were doing a brisk business in cheap, phony Harley souvenirs.  So now, after a hot day on his Harley-Davidson bike, an easy rider wearing genuine Harley boots and a Harley shirt can reach into his Harley wallet and pull out some money to pay for a Harley-Davidson wine cooler."

But the value of internationally-known brand names goes far beyond the COCA COLA on a  T-shirt or the HARLEY on a pair of boots. The pricelessness of a brand names is further underlined when one considers the other invaluable "spin-offs" available:  **One widely-recognized label can be used to successfully sell a wide variety of new products.**  So, even though Diet Coke cannibalized the long established Tab diet drink, it quickly outsold it.

And such happy families, too!  Jell-O gave birth to Jell-O Fruit & Cream dessert bars, as well as Jell-O Pudding Pops.  And how about Ivory Soap's daughter, Ivory Dishwashing Liquid, and her granddaughter, Ivory Shampoo? Behind them all, of course, was the power of recognition and respect which the entire world had **already** held for Jell-O and Ivory.  From such single brand names, whole dynasties have arisen.

## DEATH OF A BRAND NAME

In 1953, a New York inventor applied for a patent for a bottle of permanent ink applied through a felt tip, and gave it the name Magic Marker. Its company, Speedry, went public in 1959, and soon traded as high as 48 times earnings.

The company failed to capitalize on the power of the name.

But within a few years, the name became generic, with millions of people around the world...

Continued on Next Page

## GOOD BRAND NAMES -- LIKE DIAMONDS -- ARE FOREVER, AND MUST BE CHOSEN WITH THAT POSSIBILITY IN MIND!

Meanwhile, the influx of **new** names in the private label sector has become truly awesome, and they must be controlled. Indeed, if every large retailer in North America developed a private label the way that, say, Wal-Mart has done, we might end up with 3000-plus soda pops, and tens of thousands of other new products!

**Imagine if every hot dog vendor in North America had his/her own desktop version of a logo with a name as a private label.**

Giving consumers what they want is an equally important challenge for national brands, as well as for private labels. **But for private labels to pretend that they are the same quality product as a national brand is seriously questionable.** The human response to food, and to countless other products, from fashion to perfume, is exceedingly complex. The taste buds alone eventually crave the quality and familiarity of the established, accepted, widely-known "taste" to which they had become accustomed, and loved for years--even for many decades.

There is no question that, with the continuing recessionary cycles, and the endless uncertainty in the world economy, private labels **have** made strong inroads into the once-sacrosanct world of name brands.

Here's a striking number for you:  The North American President's Choice line of products has grown, in just seven years, to over 1,000 products, and the grocery chain's "No Name" line now generates some $1.5-billion annually in sales for Loblaws Cos. Ltd.

Still, the ever-increasing global market provides new territories almost daily for internationally-known brand names to take ever-stronger hold. (Don't forget the Chinese worker who was willing to shell out a month's wages for famous brand-name shoes from the U.S.)   So, by the year 2000, both American and Canadian consumption of national brands **and** private labels **combined** should be relatively smaller, compared to the brand-oriented consumption of Asia and the Far East.

It is clear that the Sam's Choices and the Saks Fifth Avenue Store Labels of the future--if they hope to grow and prosper as they have done over the past few years--will have to choose their new names very, very carefully and exceedingly thoughtfully.

asking for **any** kind of felt tip pen by using the name Magic Marker--in the grand tradition of "**ScotchTape**" and "**Kleenex**."

However, the company failed to capitalize and properly secure the name and its power--and kept on diversifying in a very large range of products.

In 1985, Magic Marker Industries lost nearly $2-million on $4.7-million in sales. It filed for Chapter 11 in April, 1986.

True, in the fall of 1991, **Business Week** noted (in a cover story on the collapse of the advertising industry) that "many Americans, brought up on a steady diet of commercials, view advertising with cynicism or indifference. With less money to shop, they're far more apt to buy on price.

And they're a lot like less likely to be smitten by Tony the Tiger or the Campbell Kids." Indeed, a survey done by ad agency DDB Needham Worldwide Inc. found that 62% of consumers polled in 1990 say they buy only well-known brands, compared with 77% in 1975. And another recent study--this one by Grey Advertising--found that 61% of consumers regarded brand names as "an assurance of quality." Not bad--but this still marked a drop of fully 6% since July, 1989, barely over a year earlier. In fact, the same study found that **fully two-thirds** of Americans interviewed declared that they were "trading down to lower-priced brands."

The question is: **Are those really "no-name" brands which they are reaching for, or are they actually newly-created products which have been rapidly accepted as brand names**, due to brand-name-like quality and wide-spread advertising behind them, just like the Chevrolets and Colgates and Marlboros of the past?

*In the long run, successful products and brands with powerful unique names will survive, thrive, and help the global consumer pick and choose the right ones.*

*The glut of so-called no-name private label brands will follow the recessionary cycle. But eventually they will die without a name on their tombstones.*

# Where Do We Go From Here?

## 12

By now, you are somewhat of an expert on naming. Please don't feel shy to share your new knowledge with your colleagues, and feel free to harrass the others in your office who are less "up" on the problems of naming. Here are some final pointers.

 *o develop a good name, management must have a system which draws together and coordinates the appropriate strategic, creative, analytic and legal resources, in order to supervise a four-stage process. Here are the steps to follow on your next naming project:*

**The first phase:** Name development is the most creative. However, there must be input that includes linguistic knowledge, historic naming references, and an update on current naming trends.

**The second phase:** This one is analytical. Judging the suitability of a name to the desired positioning in the marketplace. The process must include consideration of the appropriateness of the task at hand; measurement of the advantages of the offering, and competitive disadvantages of the name; testing its use and applications; and its potential longevity.

**The third phase:**  Here, one investigates the
name's availability.  This phase requires
adherence to a strict checklist, making sure
jurisdictions are not overlooked; that conflicts
and similarities are noted; and, as a result of
extensive and detailed searches, detailed search
reports are prepared for the company's legal
department.

**Finally, the fourth phase:**  There must be
confidence that the name has been put through
an exhaustive process, so that it can be properly
registered, and protected, through review of the
legal department's plan of action.  This requires
an audit of all search results, and analysis of
conflicts; assessment of the proprietary
component of each name; and the documentation
of a registration and protection strategy which
ensures complete and final approval of a name's
launch.

## NAMING INFLUENCES

Upon properly identifying your market positioning statement, competitive trends, and competitive names, you may consider some of the naming influences which have generated monikers throughout time:

Real Surnames:
- KRAFT
- GILLETTE
- TRUMP

Fictitious Surnames:
- BETTY CROCKER
- AUNT JEMIMA
- RONALD MACDONALD

Initials:
- IBM
- QMS
- AST

Descriptive:
- WASH & WEAR
- SILKLACE PANTYHOSE

Alpha-Numeric
- 7-UP
- 3M
- R2D2

Numeric:
- 20/20
- 1776
- NUMBER NINE COMPUTER

Short:
- X
- 1

Long:
- BIOGENAMATIX

Coined:
- EXXON
- GENTRA
- TELUS

Geographic:
- POLAR
- TEXAS INSTRUMENTS
- L.A. GEAR

Classic and Historic:
- HERCULES
- MAZDA

Dictionary:
- APPLE
- CARNATION
- WINDOWS

Pun:
- BRICK SHIRT HOUSE
- HARDWEAR CLOTHING

Humorous:
- JANITOR IN A DRUM
- ROACH MOTEL

Sentence:
- THE COUNTRY'S BEST YOGURT

Proverbs:
- CROSS YOUR HEART
- FRUIT OF THE LOOM

Slogan:
- THANK GOD IT'S FRIDAY

Foreign:
- NIPPONINCO
- DAIWOO

Generic:
- SALT
- NO NAME

It is important to note that the above influences can provide you with an endless stream of names. But be aware that the good ones are usually taken, and weaker ones will not be appropriate for your marketing strategy.

## RENAMING TO ELIMINATE
## AN EXISTING IDENTITY PROBLEM

It is true that a name is only **one** element of
the exercise, but it can eventually prove to
be a dominant factor in its continued acceptance
by the marketplace.

A name must do **more** than merely designate; if
only that were necessary, all consumer items may
just as well be numbered. In today's ever-
more-crowded, competitive, highly fluid world,
a name must function as a total message.
And that message deserves clear thought, and
must be structured as cleanly as it possibly can.
As a message, any name must compete against
thousands of **other** messages and signals.

To get through to the intended audience, that
message has to stand out from the rest. Its name
must be easy to remember; it must be subject to
minimum distortion; and it must be relevant to
the targeted receivers.

In a phrase, **its name must have power.**

To review the effectiveness of the name in question, here follows an acid test for your assessment:

According to market studies, does the name top the list in terms of recognition and awareness of what it should be identifying?

Are there any negative connotations or "new meanings" associated with the name?

Are there any potential legal threats to the name, or to other users of the name?

Is the name capable of being used globally?

Is the name being used to its full advantage in competitive marketing terms?

The above methodology is to help set course for a critical analysis. If the above process shows weaknesses in your name, then you are not only wasting much of your advertising and marketing dollars; you are also faced with a critical **name change** decision.

## EVALUATING EXISTING NAMES

However successful you are, you may not be
fully aware of the effectiveness of your name in
the marketplace.  If you are expanding, then it is
critical that you assess the global impact of your
name.  It is likely that a company which falls
short on a specific name will also find that other
current names of products and services
are either vulnerable, or ineffective.

To gain control, these organizations need to
secure a sound platform, from which an effective
name development strategy and process can be
implemented.  Here are some salient points:

Open dialogue with key corporate personnel
about current and future name issues.

Determine specific needs of name application.

Audit current  names and thoroughly review
the procedures used to develop them.

Prepare a procedural breakdown of the
planned methodology.

By now, you should have produced a two-pronged feasibility study, in that it will investigate both internal, and external, factors which are affecting the existing name.

Internally, the process should include the both the selection of separate market regions which a company serves, and the customers' point of view.

This two-pronged, multi-target approach ensures a balanced mix of data that can help executives make correct decisions based on impartial facts and a clear rationale.

The study process should be highly interactive, and use input from all corporate departments and individuals involved in the name assessment.

Information should then be pooled, analyzed, and reviewed.

This, ultimately, will produce highly-focused ideas and suggestions in tune with corporate strategies and objectives.

Furthermore, it will also isolate issues encompassing marketing, product development, strategic planning and positioning, which may have been overlooked in the past.

## ONGOING NAME DEVELOPMENT STRATEGIES

In order to be truly effective, companies have to create an infrastructure which is specific to name development. Here is a checklist of issues which an organization **must** have under its control, in order to have the capability to properly develop and manage names world-wide:

Product name management policies and procedures are firmly in place.

Key people within the organization have been placed on a naming committee and assigned specific responsibilities.

A cooperative task group is organized, which can ensure informed input on marketing, technical, and legal issues.

Existing names, whether corporate, new divisions, products, or services, are **all** regularly assessed and reviewed.

Naming trend profiles are regularly prepared for specific industries and market segments which the company is presently involved in, or may someday enter.

Naming is under ongoing development, and regular review.

If all of the above elements are **not** in place,
the organization does not have the necessary
internal resources to develop and manage names
successfully.

There are four types of situations which you will
possibly be faced with:

The need to create a brand-new
corporate/product/service identity.

You may have to reposition an existing identity.

You may not have a name problem at all, but you
wish to audit and measure the effectiveness of
your names in the marketplace.

Your company is very pro-active in naming
issues, and would like to organize a nomenclature
policy and procedures in order to prepare
yourself for upcoming global challenges.

## AND IN CONCLUSION. . .

**Naming issues have rapidly turned into strategic issues.**

Without an effective means of branding products, services, or new and merged entities, a corporate organization could quickly find itself in a costly and dangerous stall.

Ad hoc and haphazard approaches to developing naming solutions quickly come to haunt companies, even to the point of dragging them into the courts, often for many years.

Legal injunctions, negative connotations, or low market awareness are the usual consequences. In many cases, expensive marketing campaigns grind to a halt, and any market share gains are quickly negated.

The solution? Corporate executives must take a fresh look at the astonishing potential value of a name, and then commit to a process which ensures name development as a marketing priority, and not merely a loosely-managed afterthought.

For companies which introduce new products on an ongoing basis, creating an in-house naming facility becomes a viable, and probably extremely wise, option.

## SOME FINAL THOUGHTS

Remember:   A good name means power--
for a corporation, for a product, for a service, for
a magazine, for a computer, for a football team,
for a skyscraper, for a soft drink, for a
fashion label--for everything.

If a name is truly, and globally yours,
then you have true, global power.

However, if you have a mediocre name, or a
weak name, or your name is tied up in the courts,
or easily confused with others, then your
corporation is in a deep, alpha-numeric soup.

The answer clearly lies in the title
of the book you are holding in your hands:

**You must Name for Power.**

# Annotated Bibliography

# ANNOTATED BIBLIOGRAPHY

**Aaker**, David A., *Managing Brand Equity: Capitalizing On The Value Of A Brand Name* (Toronto: Collier Macmillan Canada, 1991)

**Arnold**, Oren, *What's In A Name*(1979, Julian Messner, a Simon & Schuster Division of Gulf & Western Corporation, Simon & Schuster Building, 1230 Avenue of the Americas, New York, NY 10020.) True stories of names of companies products are told, not just the choosing of the names themselves, but the development of the products they represent.

**Bogart**, Leo, *Strategy In Advertising, Matching Media And Messages To Markets and Motivations* (LincolnWood, Illinios: NTC Business Books, 1986. (A division of National Textbook company)) This book talks in part about the importance of brand image, product innovation, and the evolution of marketing concepts.

**Campbell,** Hannah, *Why Did They Name It...?* (New York: New York Fleet Publishing Corporation)

**Capitman,** Barbara Baer, *American Trademark Designs: A Survey With 732 Marks, Logos And Corporate-Identity Symbols*(New York: Dover Publications, 1976) This is a pictorial review of familiar trademarks in entertainment, leisure, sports, transportation, furniture, appliances, etc. It also includes an index of designers.

**Caples**, John, *Tested Advertising Methods* (Englewood Cliffs, New Jersey: Prentice-Hall Inc., 1979) Standard guide on tested methods of getting favourable sales results from advertising. This edition offers a solid program based on tested techniques that have sold a variety of products and services.

**Carson**, Patrick and Julia Moulden, *Green Is Gold* (Toronto, Ontario: Harper-Collins, 1991) This book is mainly a guide for companies wanting to go "Green." Designing effective labels, commercials and advertising are all discussed.

**Charmasson,** Henri, *The Name Is The Game: How To Name A Company Or Product* (Homewood, Illinois: Dow Jones - Irwin, 1988)

**Clearly**, David Powers, *Great American Brands: The Success Formulas That Made Them Famous* (New York: Fairchild, 1981)

**Cooper**, Robert G., *Winning At New Products* (Holt, Rinehart and Winston of Canada, 1986.) New products-management, new products-marketing, creative ability in business, new business enterprises. The conception, development and commercialization of a new product.

**Frand**, Erwin A., *The Art To Product Development: From Concept To Market* (Homewood, Illinois: Dow Jones-Irwin, 1988)

**Freiman,** David J., *What Every Manager Needs To Know About Marketing*
(New York: American Management Association, 1983) This book provides information on every aspect of marketing, from the basics of defining the market and positioning the product to the complexities of market research, multinational marketing, and more.

**Gershman**, Michael, *Getting It Right - The Second Time*
(New York: Addison-Wesley Publishing Company, Inc., 1990) Gershman introduces the concept of remarketing to explain the dramatic transformations of Timex, Kleenex, 7-Up and 46 other marketing failures into some of our best-known brands and products.

**Gruenwald**, George,*New Product Development: What Really Works*
(Lincolnwood, Illinois: NTC Business Books, 1985)The book discusses the name change of Allegheny to USAir in 1979. It explains the steps taken in the five-year name changing process.
The importance of brand name banks are briefly discussed.

**Hall,** John A., *Bringing New Products To Market: The Art And Science Of Creating Winners*
(New York: American Management Association, 1991)

**Husch,** Tony, *That's A Great Idea! : The New Product Handbook*
(Berkeley, California: Ten Speed Press, 1987)

**Igarashi**, Takenobu,*World Trademarks And Logotypes*
(Tokyo: Graphic-Sha Publishing Company, 1983) This book has 368 full-color pages of major International Trademarks and Logotypes that won high-acclaim internationally. Interesting background information is provided on their development.

**Igarashi**, Takenobu,*World Trademarks And Logotypes II*
(Tokyo: Graphic-Sha Publishing Company) This book is similar to Volume I, but it is an updated version.

**Jones**, John Philip, *What's In A Name? Advertising And The Concept Of Brands*What brands are and why they have emerged; defining the naming of a brand; describing how and why brands emerged in the market place.

**Kincaid,** William M. Jr., *Promotion-Products, Services, And Ideas*
(Columbus: C.E.Merrill, 1985) Sales promotion, marketing, advertising are all explained.

**Kuwayama**, Yasaburo,*Trademarks & Symbols Of The World* (Tokyo: Kahiwa - Shobo, 1987) All the works in this book were produced between 1970 and 1983.
This book mainly shows illustrations.

**Kuwayama,** Yasaburo, *Magazine Logotypes* (Tokyo: Mitsuru Takahashi, 1986) This book features an extensive collection of magazine titles having an excellent design. They were carefully selected from over 10,000 kinds of magazines which have been published in countries around the world.

**Lindberg,** Roy A., and Theodore Cohn, *The Marketing Book For Growing Companies That Want To Excel* (New York: Van Nostrand Reinhold Company, 1986) This work discusses the value of a name and the effect it may have on consumers. It explains how names like Xerox, Kleenex, and Cadillac are turning into nouns we use in our everyday language.

**Loden**, John D., *Megabrands: How To Build Them, How To Beat Them* (Homewood, Illinois: Business One Irwin, 1992)

**Matthews**, C.M., *Place Names Of The English-Speaking World*Looks at the way the British have named the places in which they have lived, both in their own islands and overseas. The result of this book is far more than a dictionary of meanings and derivations.

**Mayer**, Martin, *Whatever Happened To Madison Avenue? Advertising In The '90's* (Little, Brown and Company., 1991) A hard-hitting, incisive analysis of the health and prospects of the advertising industry. Europeon and American advertising trends are both discussed.

**McCulloch**, Gregory, *The Game Of The Name: Introducing Logic, Language And Mind* (Oxford: Clarendon Press; New York:Oxford University Press, 1989) Names Analysis (Philosophy) and Cognitive Science are discussed.

**Morgan**, Hal, *Symbols Of America* (New York: Viking, 1986) A lavish celebration of America's best-loved trademarks and the products they symbolize- their history, folklore, and enduring mystique. This extensive, entertaining and fact-filled text provides a fascinating history of these symbols and products.

**Oathout**, John D. *Trademarks: A Guide To The Selection, Administration, And Protection Of Trademarks In Modern Business Practice* (New York: Charles Scribner's, 1981)

**Olins**, Wally, *Corporate Identity - Making Business Strategy Visible Through Design* (Boston: Harvard Business School Press, 1989) Olins provides a good account of the role image has played in organizations ranging from Napolean's empire to the Confederate States of America to modern corporations such as Coca-Cola, BMW, Apple, etc.

**Pritikin,** Robert C., *Pritikin's Testament-Miracle Ads For Big And Small Advertisers, Retailers, And Entrepeneurs* (Englewood Cliffs, New Jersey:) This discusses product names, and marketplace success. Author talks about product names, and how naming a product is important, and how sometimes the name does not even relate to the product at all.

**Rosenau**, Milton, *Faster New Product Development: Getting The Right Product To Market Quickly* (New York, NY: AMACOM, 1990)

**Schonberger**, Richard J., *Building a Chain of Customers* (New York: The Free Press, 1990) This book shows how New Coke, Xerox Computers, Ivory Shampoo, and Holiday Inn Crowne Plaza all failed because of fuzzy, cluttered brand identification and unfocused marketing.

**Seiden**, Hank, *Advertising Pure And Simple(The New Edition)* (AMACOM, a division of American Management Association, 1990) This book discusses in part when you can name a competitor's name in advertisments, and the importance of competitive advertising.

**Ulanoff**, Stanley, *Handbook Of Sales Promotion*(New York: McGraw-Hill, 1985) This book discusses every aspect of sales promotion. One chapter features corporate-insignia clothing, and how to turn consumers into walking billboards by having them wear clothes with your logo.

**Wizenberg**, Larry, editor, *The New Products Handbook* (Homewood, Illinois: Dow Jones Irwin, 1986)

# Index

# A.

ABC Namebank International, 7
AGT, 7
Air Canada, 7
Alfa Romeo, 26
Allegis, 126
American Airlines, 112
Apple Computers, 66, 77, 109, 174, 176, 177
Aquascutum, 133
Atari, 120
AT & T, 97, 174

# B.

Bacardi, 190, 191
Banking on Names, 93
Bata, 75
Beatrice, 73
Bell Atlantic, 96, 97
Bell Canada, 7, 97
Bell South, 7, 87, 97, 101
Big Picture-Type Personality, 44
BMW, 191
Boeing, 75
Brand names, 189-214, 222, 224
British Petroleum, 59
Budget Rent A Car, 218
Budweiser, 190, 222
Buick, 31
Bull (Honeywell), 81, 82
Burger King, 145, 146
**Business Week**, 226

# C.

Cadillac, 34
Campbell's, 206
Campeau, Robert, 79
Canadian National Railways, 89
CARA, 7
Car names, 19-40
**Case Studies:**
  Celestica, 162-163
  Genexxa, 181-182
  Gentra, 124-125
  KPMG & Zerotime, 184-186
  Maximum, 113-115
  QUNO, 91-92
  Telus, 96-99
Celestica, 163
Chevrolet, 27, 29, 30, 171, 172, 226
**Chicago Tribune,** 91
Chrysler, 21, 26, 29, 30, 35, 37, 38
CNN, 213
Coined names, 70, 117-128, 232
Coke, 97, 190, 191, 193, 195, 198, 208, 210, 220, 221-223
Cray Research, 79
Crisco, 206
Custody of a Name, 215-228

# D.

Datsun, 33, 35
DEC, 174
DELL, 194
Del Monte, 206
De Lorean Corp., 78
Descriptive names, 70,103-116, 232

Dictonary names, 70, 130-116, 232
Disney World/Land, 213
Dodge, 31
DuPont, 156, 222

## E.

Eastern Airlines, 88, 101
Eaton, 211
**Economist, The,** 210
Edison, 72, 86
Edsel, 28
English-Only-Type Personality, 48
ESSO, 139
Ethnic slurs, 63
Everready, 206
Expotel, 7
Exxon, 66, 119, 121, 136, 221

## F.

Federal Express, 89
Ferrari, 28
**Financial World,** 190,191
Firestone, 72
Fisher Price, 207, 213
Focus Groups, 53-66, 200
**Forbes,** 191
Ford, 7, 21, 22, 26, 27, 30, 72, 77, 79, 131, 171
Foreign languages, 52
**Fortune 500,** 7, 43, 83, 100, 115, 192, 204
Fujitsu, 120
Functional names, 153-154
Future Now Incorporated, 45

## G.

Gatorade, 193
Gender bias, 52, 63
Gender-sensitive names, 144, 146
General Foods, 156, 210
General Motors, 7, 22, 30, 37
General Mills, 218
Genexxa, 7, 181
Gennum, 7
Gentra, 124, 125
Geographic names, 70, 85-102, 232
Gillette, 72, 190, 194
Gold, Naming, 151, 152
Goldrun, 185, 186
Goodyear, 86, 206
Green names, 148, 149

## H.

Hallmark, 213
Halston, 73, 74
Harley-Davidson, 222, 223
HealthTrust, 7
Heinz, 72, 194, 195,
Helmsley, Leona, 78
Hispanic market, 30, 34, 63, 119
Highs and Lows of Hi-Tech Naming, 155-188
Honda, 37
HoneyLemon, 108
Honeywell, 7, 81, 82
H & R Block, 75
Hudson Bay, 89
Hyundi, 120

# I.

Iacocca, 25
IBM, 7, 81, 162, 163, 171-174, 213
IKEA, 73
Initials & numbers naming, 171, 232
Intel, 160, 161, 190, 191
Internal naming, 41-52
INTERTAN, 181
Isuzu, 36
Ivory, 206, 223

# J.

J.C. Penny, 74, 198
Jeep Eagle Corp., 34, 35, 139
Jell-O, 156, 223
Johnson & Johnson, 7

# K.

Kellogg, 190, 191, 206
Kentucky Fried Chicken, 143, 206
Kodak, 119, 123, 132, 206, 213
Konica, 76
KPMG, 7, 184, 186
Kraft, 71, 72

# L.

Letters, feelings about, 60
Letters, power of, 144, 145
Levi's, 213
Lexus, 31
Loblaw's, 195, 225
Lowercase naming 170

# M.

Magna, 7
Marlboro, 190, 191, 196, 220, 226
Mattel, 207
Mazda, 26, 29, 132
McDonald's, 77, 146, 208, 213
Mennen, 217
Mercedes-Benz, 28, 36, 191,213, 221
MERCK, 7
Mercury, 29, 33, 131
Microsoft, 77, 156-159, 161
3M, 134
Minnova, 7
Minolta, 89, 159
Mitsubishi, 175
Molson, 7

# N.

Nabisco, 210, 212
Naming contests, 56, 60
**Naming:**
 Banking, 93
 Brand, 189-214, 222, 224
 Cars, 19-40
 Coined, 117-128, 232
 Custody of, 215-228
 Dawn of hi-tech, 164-169
 Descriptive, 103-116, 232
 Dictionary, 103-116, 232
 Functional, 153, 154
 Future of, 183
 Gender-sensitive, 144
 Geographic, 85-102, 232
 Gold, 151, 152

Green, 148, 149
Highs and lows of, 155-188
Initials & Numbers, 171, 232
Internal, 41-52
Lower case, 170
Olympic, 219
Private labels, 199
Recommendations & pointers for
  successful, 229-242
Rocky, 150
Spectrum, 129-154
Sporting, 142
Store brands, 192
Surnames, 67-84, 232
Toys, 207
Trends, 65
Vodka, 141
Wine, 141
Naming School of the 50's, 54
NCR, 174
Nescafe, 190, 196
**Newsweek,** 209
**New York Times,** 78, 203, 205
**New Yorker, The,** 164
Nike, 196, 214, 216
Nippon, 175
Nissan, 33, 35
Nintendo, 71
No-Name, 193, 195
Northern Telecom, 101
Novo-Consumerism, 189-214

# O.

O.K.-Type Personality, 49
Oldsmobile, 25, 28
Olympic Names, 219
Oshawa Group, 89

# P.

Palmolive, 194
Pampers, 190, 193
Panasonic, 120
Petro-Canada, 7, 113
Peat Marwick, 7
Pepsico, 108, 190, 195, 198, 205
**Personality:**
  Big Picture-Type, 44
  English-Only-Type, 48
  O.K.-Type, 49
  Romantic-Type, 47
  Scientist-Type, 46
  Strategic-Type, 51
  Techno-Type, 50
Pierre Cardin, 76
Playtex, 73
Political correctness, 52, 63
Pontiac, 28, 87
Porche, 75
President's Choice, 192, 195-197,
  203, 225
Private label, 199
Proctor & Gamble, 192, 209, 210
Profanities, 63
Proof Positive, MCI, 47

## Q.
Quaker Oats, 110
QUNO, 7, 91, 92

## R.
Racial associations, 63
Radio Shack, 7, 181
Ralph Lauren, 76
RCA, 108
Revlon, 73, 76, 217
Richardson-Vicks, 90, 210
Rocky names, 150
Rolex, 213
Rolls-Royce, 30, 39
Romantic-Type Personality, 47
Rowntree, 211

## S.
Sam's Choice, 192, 198, 208, 225
Samsung, 120
Sasktel, 7
Scientist-Type Personality, 46
Sharp, 120, 159
Silverrun, 185, 186
Singer, 72
SkyDome, 59, 80
Smirnoff, 211
Sony, 120
Spectrum, naming, 129-154
Sporting names, 142
Store brands, 192, 195
Store label fashions, 198
Strategic-Type Personality, 51
Stroh, 217
Surnames, naming, 67-84, 232

## T.
Talisman, 59, 60
Techno-Type Personality, 50
Teflon, 139
Telus, 7, 96-99
Texaco, 7, 82, 90, 108
Toshiba, 88
Toy names, 207
Toyota, 28, 31
Translations, 52, 63
Trump, 74, 79

## U.
Unisys, 58, 60
United Airlines, 112, 126
UPS, 213
U.S. Steel, 112

## V.
**Venture,** TV Program, 186
Vodka names, 141
Volkswagen, 38
Volvo, 35, 36

## W.
**Wall Street Journal,** 216
Wang Computer, 79
**Washington Post,** 214
Wendy's, 74
Windows, 156, 157, 158
Wine names, 141
WMX Technologies Inc., 111, 112
Woolworth's, 7
Wrigley's, 206

# X.
XEROX, 66, 119, 123, 158, 159,
 210

# Z.
Zerotime, 185, 186

## A PERSONAL REQUEST

As a student of naming, I have long been fascinated, even obsessed, with name-related information, anecdotes, stories, legal problems, translations, obscenities, cross-cultural challenges, and more.

For nearly two decades, I have gathered material of this kind, only a fraction of which I have been able to share with you on the preceding pages of this book. Still, no one person can be everywhere and read everything (even if the names we choose for our businesses, products and services had better be applicable, proprietary and acceptable everywhere!)

Which is why I now turn to you, the reader, and make this personal request:

**I would greatly appreciate any name-related business stories you come across, mailed to the address below.**

Whether these will be used in future editions of this book, or in future publications, they would be greatly appreciated.

Thank you in advance.

NASEEM JAVED
ABC NAMEBANK INTERNATIONAL.
ONE ST. JOHN ROAD
P.O. BOX 2360
BRAMPTON, ONTARIO, CANADA
L6T 3Y9